CUSTOMER
COMMUNITIES

CUSTOMER COMMUNITIES

ENGAGE AND RETAIN CUSTOMERS TO BUILD THE **FUTURE OF YOUR BUSINESS**

NICK
MEHTA
ROBIN
VAN LIESHOUT

WILEY

Published by John Wiley & Sons, Inc., Hoboken, New Jersey.
Published simultaneously in Canada.

For general information on our other products and services or for technical support, please contact our Customer Care Department within the United States at (800) 762-2974, outside the United States at (317) 572-3993 or fax (317) 572-4002.

Wiley also publishes its books in a variety of electronic formats. Some content that appears in print may not be available in electronic formats. For more information about Wiley products, visit our web site at www.wiley.com.

Library of Congress Cataloging-in-Publication Data is Available:

ISBN 9781394172115 (Cloth)
ISBN 9781394172122 (ePub)
ISBN 9781394172139 (ePDF)

Cover image(s): PAUL MCCARTHY
Cover design: © TANEWPIX289 | SHUTTERSTOCK

SKY10055492_091523

Contents

Foreword

When I moved to the United States in my early twenties, my mother bought me my first computer. She spent her entire life savings on it, because she knew it would be important for me and my career. Like every mother, she was right. By having this computer I learned how to code, but more importantly I learned how to connect with others. I was exposed to CompuServe and America Online, where I could meet with like-minded people with even the most niche interests. Bollywood enthusiasts? Check. Puzzles? Check. Rubik's Cube lovers? You bet.

The point is, once I discovered community, there was no looking back. It was the one place I felt like I truly fit in.

Community matters.

And beyond how community has helped folks personally, online communities have a huge impact on professional lives too. If you're looking for advice on how to grow in your field, what better way to get that information than from others who have already succeeded? But beyond just the professional development, companies are finally starting to connect the dots to community's impact on the broader business.

I spoke about this at the HubSpot INBOUND 2022 conference. HubSpot's main mission has always been to help businesses grow efficiently. Like all things, the means to get there have changed. It has evolved from sales-led growth to marketing-led growth and product-led growth. Now we are utilizing all of those and adding in community-led growth.

The value of community is connection. The ability to trade notes and experiences is invaluable. So it should come as no surprise that *Customer Communities: Engage and Retain Customers to Build the Future of Your Business* is, in my humble opinion, an essential read.

This book is co-authored by Gainsight CEO Nick Mehta. Nick and I first met as he was building Gainsight and working to create his own community with the Pulse Customer Success community. Over the years, Nick and I continued our dialogs at conferences and frequently on another big community: Twitter.

Right from the preface, Nick and Robin van Lieshout paint an all too familiar picture of what growing up feeling lonely and isolated was like. Maybe it's a co-founder thing? But we all managed to find ourselves through community.

Community is only becoming more important as people become more connected to technology. It aids in the crisis of disconnection.

Customer Communities is a book that should be on every forward-thinking SaaS leader's bookshelf. It doesn't just explain the ever-growing value of online communities; it provides an action plan for those looking to create a sustainable and thriving community.

In particular, I encourage you to soak in the lessons around bringing your company culture to your community. At HubSpot, we have been huge fans of transparency around our company values and approach, which helped forge the connections we see in our external community.

Community has shown me that I matter. Now it's your turn, as business leaders, to show your customers that they matter.

Dharmesh Shah
Co-Founder and CTO of HubSpot
@dharmesh

Preface

Two CEOs Growing Up Lonely

Nick Mehta

Middle school. Those two words bring anxiety to me to this day. Did anyone like middle school? Was it originally designed as some kind of torture mechanism? (Actually, my wife says she loved middle school and had friendship and joy throughout. How annoying!) For many of us, middle school brings up memories of awkward tween and teenage years, bodies changing in embarrassing ways, and struggles to fit in. Or at least that was my story.

For some reason, since kindergarten, I couldn't find my own group of friends in my Pittsburgh, Pennsylvania, suburban school. I felt weird. I felt strange. I didn't fit in. And I got a daily reminder of that.

The highest-pressure routine in middle school happened at lunchtime. Each child grabbed their tray of greasy pizza and oily french fries and had to find a table to eat at. The cool kids sat in one section, the athletes in another, and the nerds in a third. But I didn't fit in anywhere. I didn't have anyone to sit with and was definitely not brave enough to introduce myself.

So rather than suffer the life-ending embarrassment of eating alone in public, I developed a routine. I'd grab my lunch and tray and pretend that I had big things to do as I scurried outside the cafeteria.

I'd scope out the nearest open classroom—or the computer lab in high school—and endure my loneliness in isolation. I ate alone every day from age 6 to age 18.

We all carry with us the joys and scars of childhood. Despite having met tens of thousands of people in my work and in spite of routinely speaking to big audiences, the feeling of loneliness lives with me to this day. I don't know if I fit in. I don't know if people like me. I don't think they'd want to sit with me.

The memories from my school years came back to me when I thought about how I wanted to build Gainsight. We saw a big opportunity to connect our customers—who often felt alone in their own companies—into a community. And when I think about the employees of Gainsight, whom we affectionately refer to as "Gainsters," I hope we'd all invite each other to sit together at lunch.

In recent years, these feelings became amplified as I saw our children go through their own struggles to make friends and find their own "tribe." Luckily, all of them have to some extent. But I've witnessed them go through phases where they didn't think they fit in. Each time, I empathized and relived my own childhood.

One of my favorite musicals is *Dear Evan Hansen*. My wife and I watched it with our eldest child, who was wrestling with their own isolation at the time. The show tackles the issue of connection and disconnection. The protagonist laments, "Have you ever felt like nobody was there? Have you ever felt forgotten in the middle of nowhere? Have you ever felt like you could disappear—like you could fall, and no one would hear?"

But the story ends with an uplifting message. We all feel this loneliness. We all desire connection. We all want to belong. And if we find the community that makes us feel seen:

Even when the dark comes crashin' through
When you need someone to carry you
When you're broken on the ground
You will be found!

Robin van Lieshout

My life started quite disruptively: my father left when I was just two years old. The relationship between my mother and father did not hold, and I grew up without a father. I have no memories of him, and when I was finally mentally ready to trace him down in my thirties, I learned he had just passed away.

My youth wasn't always easy, and I took on many responsibilities early in my life. But I also hid away a lot—I was a shy boy. I tried to tag along with friends, but it was hard for me. Like Nick, I had no place to hang out during breaks in the school day. Most of the time I wandered around and waited until school ended.

I wasn't part of any group and didn't have many friends. I was generally pretty lonely, but like any kid I wanted to belong. I wanted to be part of a group and be accepted as a human being. I wanted to find out where I belonged and fight for that belonging. I can imagine that everybody feels lonely once in a while—both of us definitely did.

Some time ago, I was on holiday in Morocco with my kids, playing on the beach. I was pondering my own situation and personal history. I suddenly realized that this wanting to belong stemmed from my youth and had actually brought about some major milestones in my life.

One of the most important ones is that it fueled my first steps on the Internet in 1996. Growing up without close friends, I joined online groups and started chatting with others. These conversations energized me, and I came to understand the power of community. For the first time in my life, I was part of something. It gave me that sense of belonging we all strive for. And it made me feel so much better.

Next, with some basic programming skills, I started to build my own online forums discussing my passion in those days: consumer electronics. After doing that for a few years, I realized that bigger brands were also looking for technology and advice on how to build their own online communities. Those were the early days when companies were starting to provide better and faster care through social channels and open platforms. Together with my co-founder Wouter

Neyndorff, we started a company called inSided in late 2010. Our goal was to power communities for the largest brands and create that same sense of belonging I felt back in the day—but this time, for their customers.

Over the years, I have built many online and offline communities. I've come to realize that we all want to belong. That communities are essential to our daily lives.

In the meantime, I have also become less shy. Being on several stages, traveling the world visiting customers, employees, and investors has certainly helped. And the most remarkable change is that most of the time, I feel I belong.

Acknowledgments

In heartfelt appreciation, this book is dedicated to the individuals whose invaluable contributions have shaped its essence and made it possible. Their unwavering support, wisdom, and expertise have been instrumental in bringing these pages to life.

To our dear friends Haiko Krumm and Kenneth Refsgaard, your tireless commitment and exceptional skills have been the cornerstone of this project's success. Haiko was kind enough to immediately offer his support when the project turned out to be more work than we could individually handle. His energy, dedication, project management, and drive brought it to the finish line. Kenneth was instrumental in writing and rewriting large portions of this book, to make sure all stories aligned and were of the highest quality. We could not have done this without your outstanding knowledge level of communities. We are deeply grateful for both of your time, honesty, and generosity.

To our dear content experts, Aarthi Rayapura and Hannah Whalen, for your excellent writing skills and bearing with us through the end. Your guidance and skills have made this book a joy to read.

To our team of community experts, Harshi Banka, Remco de Vries, Alistair Field, Aaron Hatton, Robin Merritt, Valerie Molina, Nadia Nicolai, Erin Rhodes, Cristina Rotariu, Scott Salkin, Sebastiaan Terpstra, Bas van Leeuwen, and Seth Wylie: your expert knowledge has transformed mere ideas into tangible valuable content. Thank you for your creativity, passion, and support.

To all the remarkable individuals who graciously shared their insights and experiences through interviews, your wisdom and expertise have added immense value to this book. Your willingness to open up and share your stories has provided readers with a wealth of knowledge and inspiration.

There are numerous other individuals who supported us in this journey, including Armin Pop, Paulien Vocking, Jordan Sher, Lane Holt, Julian Lindhorst, and Alex Steinbergs. Thank you!

Most importantly, thanks to the members of the customer success community who inspired us to start this journey and motivate us to keep going every day.

This book is a tribute to the collective community efforts, unwavering support, and valuable contributions of all of you. We are honored and privileged to have had you as part of this creative journey.

Community Is the Future of Your Business

1

An Introduction to the World of Communities

Creating a Sense of Belonging

In the popular TED Talk "How to live to be 100+" (2009), author and speaker Dan Buettner attempts to tackle a question that most of us have pondered: How do we live a long and healthy life?

His Blue Zones Project is an effort to understand the parts of the world where people live unusually well and determine what we can learn and apply to our own lifestyles. Most of his conclusions about diet and exercise are reassuring but not surprising.

But his claim about the Japanese archipelago of Okinawa definitely got us thinking. Okinawa, per Buettner, has the oldest living female population in the world, the longest disability-free life expectancy, and trounces other regions on many measures, including the rates of colon cancer, breast cancer, and cardiovascular disease.

So what's in the water in Okinawa? It turns out it's the Okinawans themselves. Buettner shares the Japanese concept of *ikigai,* which translates to "life's worth" or, as the speaker suggests, "the reason you wake up in the morning." Many Okinawans have their meaning tied up in a group of others called a *moai.* This cohort is often the same collection of people you live with and laugh with from childhood to careers to centenarian days.

In short, the communities the Okinawans live in seem to literally save their lives.

Buettner isn't alone in his thought process. In *Together: The Healing Power of Human Connection in a Sometimes Lonely World* (2020), the surgeon general of the United States, Vivek Murthy, contends that the greatest epidemic endangering our health, life span, and connection isn't a traditional disease. Instead, Dr. Murthy shares volumes of research shining a light on what ails us as a society—our collective loneliness and lack of community.

None of this comes as a shock because the basis of human society and civilization is community. We left the caves and prairies and built towns and cities to be together. We formed institutions—religious, civic, educational, and athletic—founded on the idea of connection and shared belonging. As the philosopher Aristotle once said:

> Man is by nature a social animal; an individual who is unsocial naturally and not accidentally is either beneath our notice or more than human. Society is something that precedes the individual. (*Politics,* 1253a)

Indeed, the need for community is only becoming more apparent as it disappears. Dr. Murthy's book, and many others like it, point to our loneliness and loss of community in an increasingly disconnected and divided world. We didn't know what we'd had until it was gone.

Even the most cursory of Google searches show a myriad of anecdotes to reinforce this point:

- Nearly half of Americans report sometimes or always feeling alone or "left out" (Cigna, 2018).

- Loneliness has the same impact on your life expectancy as smoking 15 cigarettes a day (Holt-Lunstad et al., 2015).
- Socially isolated individuals crave company in the same way that hunger states trigger the search for food (Tomova et al., 2020).

While we'll leave the future of our governments and life span to other books written by many more experienced and educated authors, we wrote this one because we believe community is also vital to the future of business.

But what is a community, exactly? The *Oxford English Dictionary* defines it in two ways:

1. A group of people living in the same place or having a particular characteristic in common
2. A feeling of fellowship with others, as a result of sharing common attitudes, interests, and goals

In this book, we'll use the second definition. "Fellowship," based upon "common attitudes, interests, and goals," is what we believe a community is all about. Think of a personal community that you're a part of. Fellowship captures the feeling you have when you are with your people.

This fellowship is already there in your business, whether intentionally created or accidentally enabled. Your local coffee shop is a living, breathing community. Every show you watch and band you love has a business model that depends on the community of the fans. The Disney community is apparent whenever you visit one of their parks and see parents and children decked out head to toe in Mickey Mouse gear. Most modern "gig economy" businesses like ridesharing, delivery, and Airbnb are layered on top of a community of providers (drivers, deliverers, and hosts, respectively). This is community.

Each of these communities layers on a series of emotions:

- Feeling a sense of belonging: "I am meant to be here."
- Feeling understood: "People get me here."

- Feeling supported: "People want to help me here."
- Feeling less alone: "There are others like me."
- Feeling purpose: "We share a common goal."

Those might feel like lofty goals for a business book, but keep reading, and we'll share lots of examples of where this happens in business today.

Let's examine Starbucks. In his book *The Good Place* (1989), sociologist Ray Oldenburg coined the term "third place"—beyond work and home—to explain why communities like coffee shops provide connections and belonging. In the mid-1990s, Starbucks incorporated this idea into its mission: "We want our stores to be the third place." Starbucks is fundamentally a community-first business.

For business-to-consumer (B2C) businesses like Starbucks, which sell directly to consumers, the communities are apparent and vivid. You can see them as fellow shoppers in your local store or as fans standing next to you at a concert.

In this book, we will argue that the concept of community is just as foundational to the business-to-business (B2B) world, even if these communities are sometimes less apparent.

Businesses, even of the B2B variety, are fundamentally business-to-human (B2H). In the B2B world, whether we are selling software, services, or shop-floor machinery, we often spend too much time on the "B," and not enough on the "H." Human beings at your company work with, sell to, and provide services to human beings that work for your clients. Of course, both sets of people have corporate goals, key performance indicators (KPIs), and other important goals. But they are also all brilliant, flawed people trying to get through this one life we have to live.

Erica Kuhl is one of the true pioneers of B2B community. In 2006, Kuhl launched what is now the Trailblazers community at software pioneer Salesforce.com. It's now one of enterprise technology's largest, most thriving, and strategically important communities. She defines community this way:

> The coming together over some like-minded passion, whether it's a product or whether it's a service or whether it's a movement. What I'm always looking for when I'm building a community with anyone is, what is that special thing you have that can drive people together, to rally behind?

The impact is that if you are a B2B leader, community is a super-power hiding in plain sight:

- Your teammates want to belong to a community.
- Your customers want that too.
- Your partners want that as well.

Indeed, let's go back to the origins of community. When you're watching a riveting play, you feel the connected energy of the audience around you. As you root for your favorite sports team in a stadium, the cheers of your fellow fans make you feel like you're part of something. Your local religious group might embody a tradition that brings your life richness and fulfillment. All these communities allow us to feel a little less lonely in this big, anonymous world.

But these feelings don't stop when you leave your house or join your virtual meeting. People in newer or niche professions working in companies often feel alone since their coworkers may not really "get" what they do. Solo entrepreneurs or small business owners toil away, having to figure out nearly everything independently. Innovators in new technology areas feel like their colleagues around them think they're crazy. Even CEOs like us sometimes have no one to talk to.

In short, work—like our personal lives—can be lonely.

Elissa Fink, former chief marketing officer of data analytics software company Tableau, echoed this emotion-driven definition of community:

> The thing that brings people together around a successful community is a shared purpose. But I think there's also this sense of you found your people. Then I think there's an element of passion.

> This is who I am; this is what I love. There's an expression element to it, too. I also think there's a thing about achievement. There's a sense of, "I'm proud to be part of this, and I become better."

As entrepreneurs, we have founded and built our businesses with community at the core. This has shown up in multiple ways, including:

- Building the biggest community around one of the world's fastest-growing professions (customer success management)
- Creating high-energy events to bring these professionals together—growing from 300 to 20,000 attendees
- Developing software to enable business people to network and learn from each other from the convenience of their computers

We've learned across a decade of work in this area that the walls we construct between our teams, clients, and community are completely artificial. The best business communities allow their members to be their true human selves and seamlessly blend together their employees with their external stakeholders.

While Michael Corleone from *The Godfather* (Coppola, 1972) may have famously said, "It's not personal, it's strictly business," we'd argue that business—and business communities—are incredibly personal. And we're not the only ones to say that; according to one of the greatest business leaders of all time, Michael Scott of the NBC television show *The Office*, "Business is the most personal thing in the world."

As you read this book, we hope you leave as convinced as we are that community is not only a good way to grow your business—it's actually the future of what your company will do and should be deeply personal to your company's mission. But let's start with the growth part.

2

Communities as a Business Growth Strategy

The Only Sustainable Long-Term Differentiator Companies Have

While we've illustrated that the concept of community can literally extend our lives, we've also hinted that community is vital to the future of your business. Now let's explore why.

If a community is a fellowship with "common attitudes, interests, and goals," how does that translate to your organization? The core of a business is your customers. So a community around your organization starts with them. All your customers have something in common; they all bought your product or service. This means they have an implicit interest in what you offer and likely have a specific goal to leverage it.

Your organization's community extends beyond customers—it's also your investors, employees, partners, and prospective customers.

Indeed, it includes your broader stakeholders and even noncustomers (and there's a solid business reason to make them a part of your community, as we will show you later). In this book, when we talk about "Customer" Communities, we regard customers as the foundation, but this also includes the larger stakeholder group, too.

Communities Are Trending

Since 2009, the Community Roundtable has been tracking adoption of community among businesses. While business communities have been around for more than 20 years, they reported that 35% of company community initiatives have been in place for only 2 years or less, and the majority of programs do not exist for more than 4 years. This signals a huge increase in the adoption of community programs in recent years.

Bessemer Venture Partners, a top-tier venture capital firm backing global iconic brands, predicts that in the next five years, more than 50% of startups and tech companies will have functional groups and executives dedicated to community by the time they cross $5 million in revenue (Walker & Goldberg, 2022). In fact, three-quarters of the companies included in Bessemer's "Cloud 100 Index" (Konrad, 2022) have allocated resources to strengthen community efforts and over 10% of the Cloud 100 companies are currently hiring for a community role. This number jumps to over 20% for the top 50 companies on the list. Talia Goldberg, Partner at Bessemer Venture Partners, predicts the prevalence of community in companies' growth strategies will only increase in the future. "It's clear that successful companies are embracing community as part of their long-term strategies and are investing heavily in community."

But what is the reason for this? Why are companies investing more and more in communities? Let's explore some of the causes.

Customer Engagement as Leading Indicator for Net Revenue Retention (NRR)

With the rise of subscription-based revenue models, focusing on existing customers has become much more important. As a result, a key company metric—now a part of regular boardroom conversations—is net revenue retention (NRR). This metric measures how much your existing customer base grows from one year to the next (Bailey, 2021).

Gainsight's standard formula for calculating NRR is:

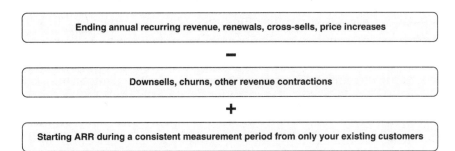

In 2022, McKinsey analyzed metric correlation with enterprise value, and revenue multiples paid for cloud companies. Next to efficient revenue growth, the single most important factor that determined company valuation was NRR. Companies who are focusing on existing customers are worth more. So it's no surprise that company boards are closely tracking and acting on this metric.

So what does this have to do with communities? In their 2020 book, *The Customer Success Professional's Handbook,* Ashvin Vaidyanatham and Ruben Rabago discovered that "the leading indicators for customer retention and expansion tend to be around the level of engagement between the client and the vendor" (p. 138). The more customers engage with your business, the more likely they stay a customer and buy more. Thus, growing your customer community— building an engaged set of customers and prioritizing customer relationships—has never been so fundamental to increasing your company's worth as it is today.

Increasing Costs Require Businesses to Be Smarter with Customer Acquisition

Customer acquisitions costs (CAC) measure how much an organization spends on acquiring new customers. It is the total cost of sales and marketing efforts to convince a customer to buy a product or service. CAC helps you discern whether you're running an efficient go-to-market organization. This is what your executive and finance teams care about. When your CFO and CEO know you're thinking about CAC, it builds trust and helps you justify budget requests.

Over the last few years, customer acquisition costs have risen significantly. Everything has become much more expensive due to privacy rules and regulations. There are also more advertisers than ever, increasing paid search and ad pricing. There's greater saturation of marketing channels and content efforts due to more competition, less customer engagement around advertising, and significant changes in buying behavior. Customers buy from companies that build products they love, but also because they feel like they are part of a community. Numerous studies have shown that people trust companies less than ever, while sources like reviews, testimonials, and peer feedback are increasingly used to inform purchasing decisions.

As a result, companies need to find smarter and more efficient ways to drive acquisition. Enter community. The drive to prioritize community comes as companies realize:

- Community is a cost-effective and owned channel that does not rely on external (paid) channels.
- Customers truly want to connect with and hear from their community.

By offering a transparent and user-generated platform, companies amplified the voice of their customers in the acquisition process and saw impressive results. Consequently, community programs have surged over the last few years.

Macro Trends Driving Community

Several more macro trends help to explain the rise of communities. After the start of the COVID pandemic, companies began looking for ways to increase their online customer engagement. Faced with travel and personal contact restrictions, companies had to get creative.

Many realized it was the ideal time to build and engage with their community online.

In addition, the core fundamentals of the Internet are changing. Web3, for instance, is an idea for a new iteration of the World Wide Web, which incorporates concepts such as decentralization, blockchain technologies, and token-based economics. The term "Web3," coined in 2014 by Ethereum co-founder Gavin Wood (Ethereum, 2023), has driven a new wave of innovation and technology investments. Instead of centralized control of data and content by Big Tech, content and decision-making power are becoming more distributed among online communities. Web3 establishes a digital highway for people to connect on their own terms to form communities that fit their needs and beliefs. The cornerstone of how these companies are built is community-led, where more value is distributed back to its users. And community isn't just a value-add for these newer companies; it's the core reason they exist.

Although there are still a lot of concerns about the decentralized web, and many see it simply as a buzzword, we strongly believe that the transfer of power to users and online communities is a fundamental shift that is here to stay. And even if we don't move to a world where everyone transacts via blockchain and Bitcoin has reached $100,000 in value, there is already widespread adoption of open application programming interfaces, more commonly referred to as APIs, which have unlocked the ability for multiple contributors to collaborate. An increasing number of stakeholders—employees, customers, and the broader community—can now meaningfully contribute to product development at unprecedented speed and scale. Even newer "Web2" companies like Airtable, Notion, and Miro have built products that fundamentally depend on community contributions. In fact, you could argue that the Open Source movement, which began in 1998, is one of the original business communities.

Companies like Linux, Red Hat, and mySQL might be considered the original innovators of the Web3 movement itself, because decentralization was already built into their core product.

The prevalence of community in companies' growth strategies will only expand in the years to come. Due to market factors like the amplified focus on net revenue retention, rising customer acquisition costs, and the accelerating influence of online communities within products, taking responsibility for this owned growth channel has never been more critical. Now that community initiatives have proven their impact in qualitative and quantitative ways, communities are starting to receive the resources and reap the rewards they deserve. Now we want to go one step further and argue that community is your only sustainable competitive differentiator in the long term.

When Product Was the Sustainable Differentiator

There's no doubt that Henry Ford (1863–1947) made a monumental impact when his company produced the Ford Model T, which would become the world's first affordable car. At the time of its release in 1908, it cost $850. As the first car to be mass-produced, its price was driven down to just $260 by 1925, and more than half of the registered automobiles in the world were Fords. Ford had perfected the moving assembly line; by 1914 one Model T could be built in about 93 minutes (Detroit Historical Society, n.d.). The demand for these cars was so great that they had to be moved out of the factory as soon as possible.

During one meeting, Ford is quoted as saying, "Any customer can have a car painted any color that he wants so long as it's black" (Ford, n.d.). One explanation suggests that he said this because he believed that he had product-market fit—the product itself was good enough as it was. It was a production era where—unlike today—power did not reside in the hands of the customer. In those days, businesses had the controlling power to dictate what they wanted to do with their product. They were not concerned about the exact wishes of the customer and felt that it was futile to cater to the customers' whims, like the desire for a specific color. It was all about the product itself, which was the market's primary differentiator. Plus, it didn't hurt that black paint dried the fastest.

We can also see the same phenomenon in the early days of the software industry. After the introduction of the personal computer (PC) in the mid-1970s, a growing software market emerged, with Microsoft as the dominant software company. Then, in the early years of the 21st century, hosted software called software-as-a-service (SaaS) emerged (nowadays likely the default operating modus for most readers). Today, there are likely billions of software applications if you include every piece of IoT (Internet of Things) software and every custom-developed software application used by businesses worldwide. Marc Andreessen, co-founder of Netscape and co-founder and general partner of Silicon Valley venture capital firm Andreessen Horowitz, famously wrote in 2011, "Software is eating the world." He predicted that software companies would disrupt traditional industries; since then, we've seen entire industries transform. The number of software companies exploded, and customers now have more choices than ever. In the last decade, the barrier to entry for SaaS has gotten so low that every software category has dozens or more players. On the peer-to-peer review site G2, the grid for any software category (including ours) includes many vendors with similar features. You could argue that technology and features are effectively commoditized.

At the same time, every company is trying to compete in this market. More software engineers are hired, and their roadmaps are full. With new product and engineering processes like continuous deployment, new features can be shipped to production multiple times per day. Companies invest significant resources in competitive intelligence, and with a smooth research and development (R&D) operation, it's easy, fast, and inexpensive to copy features from competitors.

In sum, we believe using product features as a sustainable differentiator is a race to the bottom. First and foremost, ensuring your product addresses business problems and delivers real business outcomes is imperative. It drives everything from customer acquisition, service, and support to retention and scalability. However, to succeed in business long term, companies can no longer compete on features or products alone.

Could Customer Experience Be the Sustainable Differentiator?

As we've seen, thanks to the rise of subscription-based revenue models, prioritizing existing customers has become significantly more important. It's become so critical that an entirely new profession emerged: Customer Success. Leaders and practitioners emerged to instill and operationalize Customer Success as a company-wide philosophy. Now the question is this: Is customer experience the new competitive differentiator for organizations? If it's no longer purely about the product alone, can we differentiate ourselves by delivering an improved experience?

The truth is B2B customer relationships have changed. Historically, customer relationships were personal and personalized. Personal relationships were one of the primary reasons customers bought products and became loyal to companies. We experienced this ourselves in the early days of our companies. When our products were not yet best-in-class (yes, we acknowledge those times existed!), when another new feature deployment led to significant platform downtime, or when the number of bugs was beyond the acceptable threshold our customers and teammates could cope with, we relied on personal relationships to smooth out any issues. As CEOs, we stepped in and offered our apologies to individual customers. We organized a dinner with drinks. We sang some karaoke.

However, over time, this did not scale. The number of customer accounts increased, and keeping up with every customer was difficult. New product-led customer acquisition motions emerged, where customers signed up for the product without ever connecting with someone in the organization. Plans with lower annual contract values

(ACV) were introduced, increasing volumes considerably but also challenging how we serviced our customers. CFOs started to ask questions about the increase in headcount in the customer success department. The number of customer success managers (CSMs) could not scale linearly with the growing number of customers. Based on what we have seen in the market, many technology companies still experience these challenges today.

So while investing in customer relations, customer experience, and customer success are all critical for organizations—especially to drive net revenue retention—it does not offer a long-term *scalable* sustainable differentiator.

Why Community Is Your Only Long-Term Company Growth Strategy

As we have seen, software companies are abundant today. Despite at least 50,000 technology companies already in the United States alone, new startups are emerging at an accelerated rate. Due to a myriad of technological innovations, it has never been easier to start a company. However, few survive past their first couple of funding rounds. In fact, over 90% of startups fail, and only a few make it all the way to an IPO (Hayes, 2022). Even founders with a great idea and large market potential fail in their journey, because having a great product is no longer enough to succeed in today's market.

In order to build a truly large brand, you need more. Building a decacorn—a privately held company valued at $10 billion or more in a funding event—is currently only reached by a couple of dozen companies annually. According to Chandar Pattabhiram, CMO of Coupa Software, you need "the magic combination of category and community to succeed."

Step 1: From Capability to Category Leader

All software companies start with identifying a white space capability that needs to be addressed in the market. But to take the next step in their evolution, these companies must grow from *capability to category leader.* Many companies still fail at this at a feature level. They may not have crystalized product-market fit and hence cannot create a rinse-and-repeat revenue engine. Many ideas are either too early or too narrow.

Gamification was a hot capability, but it never matured into a mandatory category. I witnessed this first-hand while running marketing at Badgeville, a company that offered the best product in a hot space. Despite having the best product in that space, it turned out that the functionality was always a nice-to-have for customers, not a must-have. And the space was always a "feature," not a "category."

Yet even after successfully identifying or creating a mandatory category and "crossing the chasm," many software companies still haven't thrived on their own. Once a category is identified, it's important to rapidly and smartly expand into relevant markets (Pattabhiram, 2019).

Step 2: From Category Leader to Category Expander

As Pattabhiram explains, companies need to focus on strategic category expansion to avoid getting stuck on their growth journey. He says that it is imperative to first focus on strategic category expansion. Avoid apples-to-potatoes expansion by trying to (expanding your category into orthogonal problem areas) in favor of apples-to-apples category expansion—thoughtfully expanding the category to become a more "comprehensive" offering in the same core functional area, appealing to the same or similar target buyers.

Pattabhiram describes Salesforce as a key example of this approach: "For example, Salesforce successfully expanded from Salesforce Automation into Customer Relationship Management (CRM). SuccessFactors also successfully expanded its category from performance management to Human Capital Management (HCM). Similarly, Coupa has successfully expanded from a focus on becoming the procurement category leader to adjacent and complementary categories, from sourcing to payments. These areas now make up the 'mega category' Business Spend Management (BSM)."

Finally, Pattabhiram describes how the process culminates in community:

Step 3: From Massive Category to Massive Community

Great product capabilities and expanding your TAM are not enough to become a successful and sustainable megabrand. Many companies successfully expand their categories and still get stuck. Once you achieve category dominance, there's one more step to reaching megabrand status.

The third most important step to become a software megabrand is *community*.

Splunk and Tableau are great examples of companies that did this right. These companies focused on building community—a tribe of customers, prospects, partners, and influencers—while also dominating their respective categories. **But you cannot wait to build a community and your tribe.** It has to happen in tandem with your early go-to-market efforts. Companies like OpenText successfully scaled to category expansion mainly via acquisitions, but they never made it to megabrand status because they didn't succeed in building a tribe.

However, many companies get community building right. Salesforce built their tribe with evangelistic marketing early in their journey to becoming a megabrand. Whether it was On Demand, SaaS, Cloud, Social, or even the Arab Summer, Marc Benioff and team aligned the Salesforce story to the relevant theme of the time and brilliantly created the feeling that they were "skating where the puck was going," and you were going to be left behind if you didn't get on this tribal train (Pattabhiram, 2019).

There are many other examples of startups that have risen to billion-dollar behemoths off the back of community efforts, from commercial open-source companies like MongoDB to popular creator-focused companies such as Figma.

In sum, you have to start building community early in your company journey and even consider incorporating it into your product. Waiting until you've achieved scale to start building your community is too late.

Community Is Fundamental to a Technology Company

In writing this book, we asked ourselves, "What is fundamental to a technology company?" The default answer might be "a product," but as we have seen, the barrier to entry for software has gotten so low that product capabilities and features are largely commoditized. We believe a software company's biggest differentiator and value proposition is the community of people who use, improve, and advocate for the product. This is why community-led growth is one of the hottest durable growth strategies in technology today.

When you buy SaaS technology, you effectively buy into a product's community of users. You are joining "the club," so to speak. Salesforce is the ultimate example of this. Since nearly everyone in technology has used Salesforce, everyone has an opinion on it. But no matter what you believe, it's undeniable that their community is massive. When you hire new heads of sales, they know how to use Salesforce. Sales reps are familiar with it, whether they like it or not. There is a community of hundreds of thousands of certified Salesforce administrators you can contract or hire at any time. And that community is constantly giving Salesforce feedback to make its products better. Moreover, community members are talking to each other about buying and using Salesforce! A huge part of Salesforce's value proposition is its community.

In late 2022, HubSpot Co-Founder Dharmesh Shah presented at the annual HubSpot INBOUND22 conference on why community matters now more than ever. HubSpot is all about helping businesses to grow efficiently, and they have witnessed the evolution of how value is created. Initially, the world was all about sales-led growth. People were doing the selling, and the *consultation* was the value add.

Sales employees discovered customer challenges and needed to connect that to company solutions. After that, we moved to marketing-led growth. *Content* was the new value add—one of the core reasons why HubSpot grew into a monumental market leader. Companies invested in content like blogs and videos, which fueled and complemented the work of the sales organization.

Next, with the decentralization of software buyers, a new value motion emerged: product-led growth. *Code* was a new value driver, and as companies aligned around the product experience, the product itself became one of the main vehicles of customer acquisition. Building on this, businesses have recognized that the ultimate goal is community-led growth, where one of the primary value drivers is *connection*. It's not the salesperson, the marketer, or the lines of code in the product. The human-first connection creates business value—for example, when people ask for advice and share open and honest experiences.

The Evolution of Value-Led Growth

Sales-Led Growth	Marketing-Led Growth	Product-Led Growth	Community-Led Growth
Consultation	Content	Code	Connection

As Shah explains, HubSpot was searching for the best way to provide the most value for their customers. They started with the product but realized great software is necessary—but not sufficient—to provide value. They also needed to provide great content, and in fact (as we will also see later in the book), you could say there was a media company embedded in HubSpot. However, the founders of HubSpot ultimately realized that there was a missing piece: community. And while HubSpot had already invested in community early on, they reemphasized and extended their commitment by launching Connect .com, a new online community for marketing professionals to help them build strong relationships with their peers and community (Shah, 2022).

The Unique Value Levers of a Customer Community

Let's explore the unique value of community in more detail.

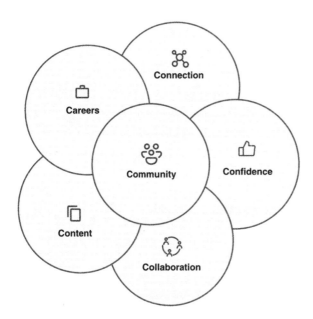

Unique value levers of community.

Connections

Community-led growth is one of the hottest strategies in technology, and the main reason is that it builds connections. We have seen that high-growth businesses create organic communities where customers link up with each other and make a connection. These connections are a relationship in which a person is linked to another person to support each other in an authentic, human process, in a way a product or technology can never achieve.

Connections are at the core of engagement between customers, employees, or partners. Passionate customers engage with new prospects, so they can understand the value of working with your company. Long term, customers help new customers with ideas on how to use your technology, and partners engage in the industry to help your company achieve value.

In addition, a vendor community greatly helps the customer from an employer's perspective. Depending on the kind of software, some companies may have only a few people using it. Having a community will help those distributed users feel a sense of camaraderie as they connect with their peers from other clients. In parallel, new hires like that their new employer—your customer—bought a software product with an extensive community (and therefore better networking and perhaps greater future career prospects).

At Gainsight, we see this phenomenon every day. Our online community and in-person events allow Gainsight admins to connect as human beings, sharing laughter, frustration, emojis, and GIFs. And very frequently, we'll hear from a customer success leader or customer success manager about joining a new software company and saying, "Thank goodness they already have Gainsight, so I'm still in the community."

Confidence

A second value add that community provides is confidence. Everyone knows that software isn't about technology—it's about achieving the outcome the technology promises. And nearly every purported outcome requires the software *and* one or more people to use it. When buyers (especially senior executives like CEOs and CFOs) consider purchasing new software, the first couple of questions that come to mind are "Who has used this?" and "Are other customers ready to vouch for this software?"

Decision-makers often seek to speak candidly with other customers and peers. Finding a vibrant user base in your community will instill confidence in them to go ahead with the purchase. The times when customers are only relying on your sales teams or marketing content are over, and confidence is a critical value driver your community can provide. And this doesn't just happen at the time of purchase. Existing customers also want to continuously have their choice of you as a vendor reinforced. By leveraging your broader community, you can continue to instill this confidence.

And beyond the senior executives and decision-makers, individual contributors making or recommending purchase decisions are spending money on behalf of their company. Unlike individual personal purchases, this gives a different perspective. Your next promotion could depend on the successful outcome of this new software project—or even more vital, your career could be on the line for bigger purchases. This results in the need for high confidence and a decent level of trust in the new vendor. This was one of the reasons why Figma, a collaborative design tool purchased by Adobe for $20 billion, was looking for the people influencing design conversations and creating a community around them to fuel the confidence for the broader market. Overall there is an aspect of who you trust when it comes to seeking guidance or making decisions: the salesperson (in a sales-driven world), yourself (in a product-led world), or trusting a community of peers and friends (in a community-led growth world).

Collaboration

In his popular book *Crossing the Chasm,* Geoffrey Moore talks about "the Whole Product." The idea is that instead of viewing your product as just the sum of its features, you should view it as everything involved with the experience that customers have with the product. It isn't just about the technology but rather about collaboration in the entire ecosystem.

For example, if it's required to hire admins or consultants to implement or use your technology, those people are part of your broader ecosystem. If there's a ready-made population of potential admins or users who are easy to hire, it makes your sale easier to close and your product quicker to implement (Moore, 2014).

As an example, Gainsight invested time and money in growing the number of professionals in the world who are certified to manage Gainsight. We tasked our customer success operations and education leaders with the charter of running our community for CS operations, to help build more Gainsight admins worldwide. Among other things such as creating a job board and a Gainsight admin Slack group with a careers section, we also launched a program called Gainsight

All under our Pulse Impact initiative. The program's goal is to train new parents returning to work in India on managing Gainsight, thereby increasing the talent pool there. As a result of all these efforts, we have radically increased the "supply" of talent, reducing the total cost for our clients. By building our collaborative community ecosystem around us, we reduced the time it takes to source talent, decreased the total cost of ownership of our software, and reduced time to value while simultaneously growing an army of advocates.

Similarly, Salesforce created this huge developer ecosystem around their company in other businesses. Instead of people leaving the organization and becoming a Microsoft developer or going to Oracle, they were so connected to each other and the product that they wanted to transition to companies already using Salesforce. And based on their experience, many even convinced companies to switch to Salesforce. This way, Salesforce kept collaborating with a large group of people, creating this sticky ecosystem and Salesforce fans for life.

But building a community ecosystem goes beyond a partner network. It's about connecting with other technology vendors to integrate natively with each other's technology stack. It's about a developer network that can build extensions on top of your core product. It's about the dense relationships with investors, which can fuel your next step in growth. Community thinking provides the value driver to build collaboration in your ecosystem.

Content

The fourth value driver is content. And while company-owned content has been around for ages, it has not always been sufficient enough to satisfy customers' needs. In a typical company, only a handful of people are tasked with creating content for customers—including both marketing content to convince prospects to become customers or "post-sales" content to educate and inform existing customers.

At the same time, your broader community is continuously developing content, but maybe not always explicitly in writing or in a readily available and reusable format. Customers are talking about your product: discussing workarounds, new feature ideas, best practices, and communicating their experiences to others. We would argue that most customers know your product better than most of your team members! So your community sits on a lot of user generated content, which companies could leverage at scale to drive outcomes. And all this content is created with an "outside-in" view instead of an "inside-out" view, making the content more relevant and valuable most of the time!

As we will discuss in later chapters, an online community can act as an effective central hub of knowledge for documentation, training, ideas, and best practices—essentially, everything required for customers to get the most out your product. It could be the digital extension to your customer success and product teams, providing valuable tips and information to new customers. Most importantly, though, it serves as an easy way to connect with other users while learning to use the product and share best practices, elevating all customers' overall knowledge.

Another form of content includes product ideas and customer feedback. How does a software company get better? We'd posit the only long-term answer is that you have a committed set of clients. They give you feedback (sometimes nicely, sometimes harshly) on how to improve. And good vendors listen. But without a community, whom do you listen to? We have received and shipped hundreds of product enhancements requested in Gainsight's Customer Success product based on our community's passionate feedback.

To put it another way—if all of your customers combined cannot create the content your company and your entire ecosystem need, who else can? Therefore content, especially at scale, is another unique value driver of community.

Careers

The last value driver is careers, a unique lever for communities that you might not expect. In the end, we believe that all businesses should be human-first companies. Working in a software organization is not just about generating profit, creating shareholder value, and acquiring new customers. Yes, prioritizing these goals is essential, but it's also about the individuals behind them. Like you and us, these individuals care about personal progression, learning, gathering knowledge, and developing skill sets. And while 50 years ago you might have done that at one company for your entire career, work mobility is now more pervasive than ever before. If your job, profession, or industry has built out a robust and accessible community, it's also easier to leverage your experience in different contexts. The community can facilitate the role transitions of people in the same field, because it's easier to see the ecosystem, have transparency, and have the ability to connect with others. Within these communities, you cultivate relationships that could result in future career opportunities. Ultimately, the community can also help us thrive in our careers.

However, having these career opportunities is also beneficial for the companies involved. We talked about our efforts in increasing the number of professionals worldwide certified to manage Gainsight. We are actively looking to expand this community, continuously facilitating career opportunities via job boards and distributing open career opportunities for the broader customer success community. By fostering our community, we hope to contribute to personal careers and genuinely create success for all.

Community as Strategic Priority

Historically, you could say that for many businesses, purchasing a product was just about buying software. But over the last 15 years, buyers have realized that the community around a vendor is a huge part of its value proposition. Without a community, a product is just another piece of software. Ultimately, it's the people who develop and use it that make the software valuable.

Our goal with this book is to show you why and how community becomes and remains a strategic priority for your organization. This book is written for a diverse set of teams because we believe buy-in on community principles from various company leaders is critical for its success. We are eager to show you how to tie the community closer to your business and integrate it into your strategy. With our 25-plus years of experience, we aim to distill the core success factors into logical building blocks. We want to be as precise and prescriptive as possible in this endeavor.

Before we dive into the 10 laws of successful community building, we want to show you how it translates to value for different teams inside an organization. The following chapter will examine how every department can benefit from a next-generation community.

3

How the Next Generation of Communities Drives Success

The New Company-Wide Strategy to Drive Net Revenue Retention

Humans have succeeded largely by cooperating and collaborating within communities. In the modern age, where many of us are less connected to the people directly surrounding us, the Internet has opened up the opportunity for humans to once again find their community of like-minded individuals.

It's not all that different in business—companies have discovered the value and power of bringing customers together, resulting in the birth and growth of business communities over the last three decades.

The Evolution of Business Communities

Starting with the early dawn of computer-connected networks and the Internet, there have been online communities. Since that time, these communities have grown through massive changes and multiple iterations, mediums, and forums. Let's explore these phases and their significance in where we stand today.

Phase 1

The older readers among us might remember the original Bulletin Board System (BBS). Before broadband Internet was widely available, you had to dial into these networks with your PC modem (yes, those were tough times!). The BBS offered a simple way to post messages between users, just like a traditional offline bulletin board found on the walls in many public spaces. Through the 1980s and early 1990s, BBS was the primary form of online community.

In the late 1990s, after the World Wide Web arrived and Internet access was more commonly available, these messages were transformed into protocols and applications like Internet Relay Chat (IRC) and ICQ, one of the first text-based messengers to reach a wide range of users. In early 2000, popular community websites emerged like Digg.com, a social news website allowing people to vote up or down for pieces of web content—revolutionary at the time.

These initial social and community initiatives were mainly about individual people engaging with each other online, sometimes with a business purpose.

Phase 2

In the mid-2000s, with the arrival of social media, companies recognized that they needed to be more present on the Internet beyond just having a website. Companies like Facebook, Reddit, Twitter, and Instagram emerged. Also, some early forum-based solutions popped up, which catalyzed the earliest enterprise communities.

These were a fascinating few years where companies (especially marketing and sometimes customer support teams) invested in social media programs. Since customers started to engage heavily on different social media platforms, companies had to keep up with social support and listening programs. A reactive support motion primarily drove this era, and social media was viewed as just another channel.

Companies like Jive and Lithium were early advocates of enterprise communities and acquired many B2C brands, like telecom operators, as their customers. With the widespread adoption of mobile and later smartphones, online engagement took off, and providing online customer support was key for businesses. Increasingly, organizations had a "face" for their brand, as real employees served as their spokespeople and had real (albeit reactive) conversations with customers online.

Today

Since then, most companies have abandoned their early social programs and have now integrated core social media initiatives into their marketing organization. Social media channels are now firmly established as hugely impactful pathways to reach and develop audiences (i.e., connecting with a large volume of customers and prospects), and thus a key channel for advertising and broadcasting marketing campaigns. The rising popularity of online platforms and social media has lessened the influence of traditional media, and most companies have shifted advertising dollars significantly.

Simultaneously, companies have increased their spending in community programs over the last 5 to 10 years, as we learned in the previous chapter. While social media engagement can be shallow and less likely to forge lasting relationships, communities are facilitators of ongoing, deep customer engagement. It has shifted from a mere customer support initiative to an engagement channel integrated throughout the customer journey, involving a diverse set of teams like product, customer success, sales, and marketing. The use cases for communities have extended to include networking, ideation, engagement, sharing of best practices, thought leadership, and advocacy. Community has moved from a tool or platform to a strategy—one that creates space for a group of people to come together and feel a sense of belonging.

Community has evolved to benefit more internal stakeholders at companies. An interesting analogy is the rise of customer success, which is the concept of achieving business growth by adopting a customer-focused approach. Customer success is a company-wide philosophy; every team needs to participate in improving the customer experience. Customers usually don't care how you are organized internally; they judge the whole package or overall experience. Similarly, when customers engage with your community, they expect to engage not only with one specific department but also with your organization as a whole. So the entire organization needs to be aligned on driving customer success and building your community!

Despite the clear evolution of online communities, not everyone in business understands what community encompasses and its potential to drive growth. Let's take a look at the old way of looking at communities, and contrast it with how we see the next generation of communities.

The Old Perception of Communities

B2C support communities were the pioneers. The sheer volume of support tickets provided a great case to start this first wave of enterprise communities. In the early days, communities were used to deflect support tickets. It was a reactive, tactical play. Communities began as simple forums where customers could help each other.

It was sometimes seen as a nice-to-have—especially with the rise of social media—when businesses found it hard to keep up with online chatter about their brand.

Companies wanted to control all online interactions and messages. In fact, we vividly remember an executive meeting with a prospect in 2008 with one of the largest telecom operators in Europe. During the course of several months, our teams had put together a plan to launch an online community before it was discussed with executives for final approval. In that meeting, one of the senior VPs got up and exclaimed, "We are not really giving customers a place to *complain* about us under our own brand, are we?" Of course, by then, social interactions were already surging, and customers had many options to "complain." Not being a part of those conversations was and is just sticking your head in the sand.

While support is still important and relevant, it does not unlock the broader value, and customers expect more today. Focusing exclusively on support is an old way of looking at the value of communities.

According to Erica Kuhl, an early community pioneer at Salesforce.com, "Historically, support was the fundamental use case, and now I won't let that happen anymore because I think that's shortsighted. It's not the best use of money, time, energy, and resources for the community to sustain in the long term. It has to be more than that."

Salesforce adopted an open and transparent approach to community-building. As Erica explained, "It was great for me to always be able to have leadership say, 'We're keeping this public. We have every one of the community ideas completely public.' And the talk track they would have is, 'If the competitors think they can do it better, they should do it because we're all in this together. We're all in it to be better citizens and to build better software to enable growth in our companies. Go for it.' And the reality is, they never could. They never did."

Historically, internal ownership of communities has often moved around, as many teams did not know what to do with this new phenomenon. A single individual often drove communities as a kind of renegade program. It was perceived as a standalone, siloed project, often with little alignment or integration into the overall company strategy. If the early advocate or business sponsor left the company, there was little guidance or handing over of knowledge to continue to grow a thriving community. Best practices and benchmarks were hardly available, and community teams were small and reliant on heroics.

Another old way of looking at communities includes the belief that it's hard to prove the ROI to the business. At one point, community practitioners struggled to provide relevant insights and data to internal stakeholders, which diminished their role because they weren't taken seriously. Key performance indicators (KPIs) were based on the number of members, page views, or community signups. And if practitioners were focusing on business results, they were looking almost exclusively at call deflection as ROI. This aligned with the thinking in 2005–2015 that enterprise communities primarily functioned as customer support. It was oriented within the broader business model thinking, which still focused on old funnel models and only reactively on servicing customers post-sales. Although certain KPIs around the quality of customer support existed, support organizations were perceived as cost centers—and the approach to community echoed this. Yes—can you believe that customer retention was not the hottest topic in those days? In fact, "customer retention" as a search term has more than doubled on Google over the last few years!

It was not just the support use case that was limiting; it was also traditional thinking around community platform technologies. For example, consider the concept of "registration" for the community. This implies that customers need another login in addition to one for the product. To prevent this, we would assume customers are already a record in the company's CRM system or product entitlement database. At the same time, community practitioners have to maximize their efforts to get people to register on a platform, the same people other teams already have in their database, wasting a lot of time and effort. And we are not talking about single sign-on (SSO) here. Of course, having one login account for all company-related systems is great, but that does not dismiss the fact that you are not in the community before you have actually registered—with or without SSO.

This siloed approach resulted in an emphasis on the number of community members and related activity metrics. Community teams needed to fight for customers' attention and were judged by how many existing customers created an account in a siloed community environment.

This does not mean members, page views, and activity are not important. It can determine the health of your community, but it cannot start or stop there. In fact, you could also argue that a group's quality does not always improve if the group is larger, so you could debate if the size of registrations should be a key goal. In many communities, we've seen that the number of registrants is only a drop in the ocean. If you compare registrations with the number of overall customers, it's usually a small percentage.

This brings us to another old way of thinking, that it's all about active participation on the platform. But in reality the number of questions asked on your online community will only be a small percentage compared to the total customer support questions you get. And that's okay, as we will soon explain. In the end, the focus on "superusers" and "peer-to-peer" in the context of answering as many community questions as possible in order to reduce headcount is not materially relevant for companies. Yes, some customers help out in your community and potentially offer free support resources for your organization. However, for larger organizations, the cost savings in direct headcount is usually not material to use as a business ROI argument. This does not mean we should not foster and grow superusers and advocates. There are plenty of business reasons to do that, but the goal of reducing headcount isn't one of them.

We believe we need to step out of our traditional way of thinking around communities and start to look at it differently.

How We See the Next Generation of Communities

How *should* we look at communities? Before we can answer this question, let's return to the emergence of customer success. As we said earlier, focusing on existing customers has become way more important with the rise of subscription-based revenue models. Where customer support was all about a reactive type of motion, customer success promises a more proactive value-added approach toward customers. Companies realized that it's also their job to make customers wildly successful with their product and started to invest in it. With this move from customer support to customer success, the strategy, goals, and use cases of communities also expanded.

In their "Market Guide for B2B Customer Community Platforms,"[1] technological research and consulting firm Gartner® found that companies with an "existing community are typically evolving the community to move beyond a support forum to drive a broader set of use cases including customer adoption, engagement, advocacy, and growth." One of the key findings is that, "While online customer communities used to originate within customer service, they are now supporting several use cases across the customer journey to scale customer as well as prospect engagement digitally."

In the evolution of the customer community use case, Gartner mentions the concept of "Community everywhere," where they predict that "platforms have moved from offering experiences via a hub model with a single entry point to inviting community interactions via multiple entry points." The report states, "Companies are looking to embed the community experience not solely via a login to a community 'site' but natively across the entire customer journey. 'Community everywhere' means the ability to embed and interact with the community in any customer digital channel and within the product, including the website, on social media, through events, via a customer support chatbot, and through messaging channels. Community everywhere means truly engaging with the community in two-way interactions without having to leave that channel, not just a link or a push of community content into that channel."

---

[1] Gartner, "Market Guide for B2B Customer Community Platforms," Maria Marino, Michael Maziarka, Chad Storlie, October 10, 2022. GARTNER is a registered trademark and service mark of Gartner, Inc. and/or its affiliates in the U.S. and internationally and is used herein with permission. All rights reserved.

Market Analysis:Customer Community Use-Case Evolution

Community is a fundamental layer on top of your business that facilitates all your engagements with customers, wherever they are and whenever they want. It's core to your business strategy, because there is no business without customer engagement.

Compare that with customer relationship management (CRM), a strategy companies use to manage interactions with customers and potential customers. We usually refer to a CRM *system*, a contact and sales management tool. Over 90% of companies worldwide use a CRM system, a proven underlying strategy and technology that facilitates *internal* business operations. Community is the strategy and technology to support the *external* part of the business—your customers. It's the glue between your organization and your customers and acts as a layer of engagement and content that builds and supports your business. It should support your existing processes and KPIs and should not be viewed as a different destination with standalone goals. It's about building your brand, and community is at the center of what you do by connecting to your customers.

Another way we should look at communities is how much scale it brings. We pointed out earlier that the number of questions asked in your online community will only be a small percentage compared to the total number of customer support questions you get. And that's alright because we should not judge the effectiveness of a community by its direct contributions. It's all about the *indirect* effect these platforms have. It's not about that one question that gets answered; it's about the 200 people that read that specific answer once it's available in your community. It's about the content you build up over time and the relationships you build around your organization. Basically, it's the compounding interest—the interest you earn on interest. The more content you have, the more trust it builds, creating that sustainable advantage.

Jillian Bejtlich, experienced community builder and leader currently building out the Calendly community, says, "All community posts with an answer in our community get, on average, 234 follow-up views. That doesn't mean that 234 people also directly have their questions answered, but it does mean that some percentage of those 234 people didn't go and submit a ticket. So even if we were to say, 20% or 30% of that, that's still a decent amount."

And this is relevant not only for questions asked in your community but also for all other types of community interactions. Melissa Gurney Greene, director of community development at HashiCorp, says, "The HashiCorp User Groups (HUG) program spans the world in 53 countries with over 36,500 HashiCorp users across 145 chapters. For every community speaker that organizes a HashiTalk, there's another 50 or 100 passive community members." If we would only judge the community based on the *direct* number of community speakers, it will not consider the *indirect* scale you achieved. Another example is engagement on Slack—it's not about those 100 individuals without customer engagement Slack messages; it's about the 10,000 people who read your community posts in the next six months (something that will not happen on Slack as a platform). And in fact, the best communities scale faster than your customer base. That means when customer growth is expanding, for example, times two year-over-year, active community growth should be expanding at least at the same rate, if not faster.

And sometimes, it's just about unscalable initiatives. For example, while you don't need a review from all of your customers, you can source reviews for the peer-to-peer review site G2 from your most loyal community members. Or, while those superusers in your community might not be needed to reduce internal support headcount, they can provide you with that single unique workaround your support team could not develop, offering a solution to tens of other customers as well. Or finally, it may be that a single multi-million enterprise customer attended your executive event and decided to renew your service because they *want to be part of the community*. They felt that sense of belonging with your company.

We should also be looking at communities differently from a technology perspective. CRM and customer success management systems like Gainsight should be closely integrated into community technology to facilitate a seamless customer experience. Customers who are already in your CRM are automatically part of your community (as well as prospects—remember that in this book, we talk about customers, but this also includes your broader stakeholder group). No need to register separately, as they already signed up as a customer or registered themselves as a prospect when they downloaded your e-book or visited your event. Account, customer journey, and customer health data should influence a personalized community experience. Executive dashboards should be available to clearly show a 360 view of each person and views on aggregated business outcomes.

As we will see in one of the community laws later in this book, communities need to be seen as a central customer hub for all content and engagement. All customer-related content should be provided in a single place to provide a seamless customer experience. For example, all your roadmap updates, event content, and customer education programs are part of your community and not on separate journeys and platforms. Companies must provide one layer of training and enablement and create that broader self-service experience customers expect. This holistic view of communities requires community platforms to evolve into supporting the next generation of business needs.

The chart seen here summarizes the core differences between the new and old ways of thinking about communities.

Old Way	New Way
Renegade programs	Company-wide program
Customer support	Customer success

(continued)

(*continued*)

Old Way	New Way
Support KPIs/call deflection	Net revenue retention
Tactical play	Business strategy
Siloed standalone community site	Integrated in customer journey
Reactive	Proactive and personalized
Focus on KPIs like # members	Focus on business results
Focus on direct contributions only	Focus on scaling community
Loosely integrated	Integrated in CRM and CS platforms
Fragmented content experiences	Centralized content
Transactional engagement	Sense of belonging
Primarily content-focused	Human-first and people-focused

In this new way of looking at communities, all departments benefit. Let's dive into how to do that in the next chapter.

4 | A Community for Customer Success, Support, Marketing, and Product Teams

How Every Department Can Benefit from a Next-Generation Community

As we've already touched on, the use case for support organizations to leverage communities is well established—it was the primary driver of the first wave of enterprise communities. Even in today's leading customer success communities, support is often still one of the most important drivers of community value.

How Support Teams Benefit from Community

Consider a customer's options when looking for an answer to a question. For questions about a product or service, it's usually possible to reach out to a support team via a one-to-one channel, and for urgent questions that will likely be the best thing to do. However, many questions are less urgent, and the one-to-one channels can be inconvenient when you have to deal with opening hours, waiting times, or even the risk of encountering a dreaded chatbot or interactive voice response (IVR) menu. Instead, many will choose to first look online. Research firm Forrester already concluded several years ago that the preference for self-service channels has long overtaken the preference to ask for one-to-one support.

A self-service experience usually starts by browsing through available resources or simply searching via Google. This latter option is, in fact, the most likely first step a customer will take in many situations. With as many as 8.5 billion daily searches (Marmon, 2023), Google has become our collective instinctual first step—and as we've all experienced, it will often surface self-service and community-driven content as the most relevant result. As a customer told us recently, "When I have a question about Salesforce, I always Google it, even though I'm familiar with their community and know that Google will send me there anyway."

One of the main reasons communities are such content powerhouses is that questions are more specific than what is described in official documentation, chatbots, and FAQs. Over time, these questions and answers serve as long-tail content that covers far more ground than any official resource ever could. That's because a community is often the only place to answer a narrow question. This has additional advantages. Assuming that the community is public, all of this content will be continually crawled by search engines like Google, making it instantly available to the next person with the same question. This is beneficial as customers post questions in simple, everyday language they use themselves instead of industry jargon used internally within your organization. It increases findability by other customers because these relatable phrases are likely closer to the words they may search for.

Clearly, a powerful element of scale is at play here as community content grows. But in addition, communities also tend to invite questions that simply can't be answered by an FAQ or a chatbot. Not all customer queries are a simple how-to questions that can be answered with a standard response.

Customers are looking to get a specific job done, which can go beyond the workings of your product. For example, when someone is looking for advice, a community can house responses from other customers that may be more helpful and trustworthy than the official content or the advice of a support agent. Or when looking for a best practice, the community will be the better place to go as multiple perspectives from peers can be shared and discussed. From the support organization's perspective, this frees up agents' time and resources to focus on the tickets they can best answer. Ditte Solsø Korsgård, community program manager at Sonos, says, "Only 50% of our community questions are related to solving a problem; the rest are related to getting how-to guidance and advice." In this sense, the scaling power of communities for support is more than just a matter of deflecting tickets; it's also about giving the support team the focus to handle the types of questions that they're most qualified to answer.

Finally, we have to touch on the unparalleled power of communities in terms of peer-to-peer support. The justification for the first wave of enterprise communities was centered around knowledgeable customers helping each other and delivering majorly cost-effective support. Everything from gamification systems to superuser programs were designed to maximize the participation of the community's most knowledgeable members. Very often, even in extensive communities, this was just a handful of users who tirelessly answered the majority of questions.

As we move beyond this mindset, we still hold peer-to-peer dynamics in high regard but now see it in a fresh light. Our top community members are often our most valued customers and advocates. We build lasting relationships with them. For support organizations, the results continue to speak for themselves. In our work with technology giants like Unqork we routinely see the vast majority of questions answered by nonemployees. As Danny Pancratz, the community director at Unqork, says, "While it's not necessarily about reducing headcount, our support teams can help more customers without us needing to increase our support headcount at the same pace. Also, as our community solves so many of the simpler queries, our support team is able to focus on higher-impact activities and tickets only they can solve." This is a great way to build an efficient business and control your cost of goods sold (COGS), the direct costs you incur in building and running subscription-based software services.

Jillian Bejtlich, Community lead at Calendly and former Zapier director of community, previously ran the Zapier support community. Zapier, a workflow automation company, has many different use cases for their product, given the technical possibilities of their product. They achieved an 85% reply rate within 18 hours on all of their questions in the community. Community members can't answer all questions, and those are pushed into an internal Airtable system that uses an algorithm to figure out what needs to be addressed first. Bejtlich explains: "We also look at our analytics almost daily to figure out how to build the right proactive and reactive content. Our goal is to see if trends are starting to emerge, which might not even be a thing—or worse, an incident—yet. We notice it before everyone else, try to react to it, get the documentation out there with really, really strong search engine optimization (SEO), and ensure that we have the right knowledge at the right time in the right place for customers."

How Customer Success Teams Benefit from Community

Customer success is still a relatively new discipline, yet we increasingly see a trend of community programs driven from within the customer success organization. The first wave of enterprise communities focused on large-scale reactive problem-solving for large B2C companies. Still, as we've seen above, communities can be even more powerful regarding knowledge sharing in a broader sense: best practices, guidance, and advice—in other words, how to get good results and extract *value* from a product or service—and inspiration around what is possible. This is all very close to the heart of what customer success teams do with their customers daily, and communities are unique in opening up possibilities for this kind of knowledge sharing at scale.

A simple example that illustrates why customer success teams prioritize community programs can be found in what is probably the most common question that customer success managers receive: "I want to talk to someone in a similar situation to me." As a customer success manager you can, of course, introduce customers to each other. It's a great practice, and the knowledge-sharing in a call between two customers is invaluable. But with a community program, this suddenly becomes possible at scale through the facilitation of user groups or simply the organic discussion of best practices that happens in the community.

In the last few years, there has been increasing focus on the idea of digital customer success. Like support organizations looking for ways to manage costs, customer success organizations now identify durable growth as a primary organizational goal. Part of this often means segmenting customers as a relatively higher or lower touch, depending on package or contract value. In many cases, a digital customer success program will position the community as the primary resource for lower-touch customers who may not have a dedicated customer success manager. This is a sensible thing to do, yet there is a pitfall here in thinking of the community as only for the lower-touch segment. In practice, we've observed among our customers that the community is a powerful resource for all segments. With the lower segments, support and education within the community may be the primary resource available. However, in the end, all customers benefit from connecting with others in the community, and also customers in the higher segments are looking for ongoing education, advocacy, and networking. Also, for these customers finding their information and answers in the community frees up time to have more strategic and high-impact conversations, for example, during executive business reviews (EBRs) and other check-ins. For these reasons, the teams of customer success operations (CSOps) are increasingly looking at communities as a way to roll out digital-led programs and scale self-service in general across all segments.

Something that all customer success teams value for all of their segments is an understanding of the level of engagement of their customers. Engagement is a broad term, and it can include product adoption, open rates of emails, attendance at EBRs, and many more potential markers of retention and churn risk. Communities offer an additional level of understanding and a way to directly influence and grow the engagement of customers. Knowing that customers are visiting the community, asking questions, and sharing their feedback arms the customer success team with deep insights into the health of their accounts. Increasingly we see community engagement metrics feed into health scorecards in customer success platforms like Gainsight. From our own work with hundreds of B2B-focused technology companies, we know that it's possible to engage anywhere from 10% to 50% of customers monthly in a community, creating insight for the customer success team and indirectly influencing net retention outcomes.

How Marketing Teams Benefit from Community

We don't see communities that are owned and driven primarily by the marketing organization as often as other organizations, like support and customer success, but there are many good reasons for marketing teams to get involved and to be excited about the value they will get from a community program.

There was a time when a purchase might be made largely based on a marketing campaign, a sales pitch, or a business application, a response to a request for proposal (RFP). Now, however, regardless of whether we're buying a vacuum cleaner or purchasing a major new SaaS platform, it is almost certain that we will seek out the opinions and perspectives of friends, peers, and existing customers. Many studies show that we're over 90% more likely to buy from a brand that's been recommended to us. This is where a community can be a powerful generator of thought leadership and recommendations from a company's most loyal customers. The community becomes an open and transparent channel for new customer acquisition at a fraction of traditional customer acquisition costs.

While word-of-mouth recommendations are an obvious and important asset for all companies, the fact is that communities can deliver value through the marketing life cycle. All of the content created in a community tends to drive powerful search engine optimization (SEO) results, funneling additional traffic into the on-domain site via the community, inevitably drawing a portion of those visitors onward to the product and other pages on the site. Community content becomes a bottomless source of topics and opportunities for ongoing content marketing.

In the consideration and purchase phases of the life cycle, the community continues to add value by generating user-generated recommendations and reviews. These are easily findable and available in the community itself. Still, a savvy marketing team will ensure that these user-generated insights are surfaced across other key touchpoints in the journey. In fact, one of the most powerful effects of a customer community is that it becomes a place where you develop deep relationships with loyal advocates. This opens up opportunities for collaboration and partnership by creating content such as case studies and webinars. This is gold for the marketing team while simultaneously an opportunity to develop careers for the advocates and a new way to position themselves as thought leaders—a true win-win.

In short, a customer community offers the unique possibility of harnessing the crowd's wisdom to generate authentic and trusted customer recommendations and believable proof points of value. Many of the themes we've discussed apply to the full post-sales journey. This is community-led growth where the product's users serve as advocates and a support network for other would-be customers—something no email or paid search campaign can compete with. If companies can harness active community engagement and get millions of people banging the drum about their product, they can sit back and focus more on building rather than selling.

Shopify, an e-commerce platform for online stores, took this engagement and broader thought leadership to a new level. Shopify became a verb, and Shopify became the "Kleenex" of e-commerce, where the brand name became the industry product. They created a thriving product community around entrepreneurship and starting their own business, and it was much broader than just Shopify itself, becoming a movement around small business and entrepreneurship and inspiring the rebels with their brand taglines. They have built a continuously evolving community and ecosystem that remained critical for them throughout their journey.

How Product Teams Benefit from Community

The days when technology companies could create products without listening to customer feedback along the way are long gone. Purchasing decisions today are heavily influenced by peer recommendations and user-generated reviews—for instance, the power of G2 reviews for B2B SaaS products. This means that it is essential for product teams to actively engage in a product feedback loop. In practice, however, this is often easier said than done. Many technology companies struggle with fragmented information flows involving multiple customer data sources, leading to a painful lack of aggregated feedback and making it challenging for the product team to prioritize their roadmap or understand what is limiting product adoption from a customer point of view.

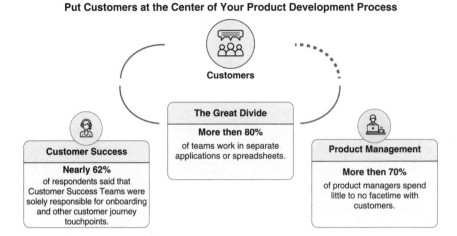

Put Customers at the Center of Your Product Development Process

Customers

The Great Divide

More then 80%

of teams work in separate applications or spreadsheets.

Customer Success

Nearly 62%

of respondents said that Customer Success Teams were solely responsible for onboarding and other customer journey touchpoints.

Product Management

More then 70%

of product managers spend little to no facetime with customers.

These challenges have led leading technology companies to start harnessing the power of customer communities to create centralized spaces where product feedback can be captured in the form of ideas. Rather than generating streams of individual pieces of feedback, the community becomes a place where members can collaborate and vote on the ideas that have been shared, creating a highly scalable and efficient path to aggregating and surfacing what truly are the most wanted features. Support and customer success teams will then often actively promote the community as the central place to share feedback, solving a lot of the fragmentation issues and finally putting an end to the endless emails and spreadsheets full of individual non-aggregated feedback.

The power of a one-to-many channel is that it opens up the possibility to efficiently and scalably collaborate directly with customers by responding with comments or clarifying questions. In fact, while buy-in from the product organization is essential for community feedback programs, the most effective ones are owned by the product teams themselves, with product managers directly engaging in the community. This closes the feedback loop in an unprecedented way, creating the possibility of a direct and trusted relationship between customers and the product team that simply isn't possible through any other channel.

Mary Poppen, customer intelligence strategist and board advisor at Involve.ai, a platform providing early warning signals for customer health, believes that product teams could benefit more than they are today. "By connecting the voice of the customer in the community, you can engage the customer and the product team directly in a scalable way. Customers can see the visibility of what other customers are requesting, so it keeps many of the enhancements more valid to the roadmap. Being roadmap-consistent for most customers is important, instead of customers (especially enterprise customers) requesting one-off enhancements. A community can facilitate that process."

OpenSpace, a company selling software to the construction market, has built an authentic community led by Nikiya Crisostomo as head of community. Their group of innovators are OpenSpace fans and champions, but they also help each other grow in their careers. Jess Lam, director of product, engages the whole internal product management team in the community. "We're a very customer-centric organization, and for our product team, that means speaking to many customers. However, there's only so many customer calls you can do in a week. And especially with our customers, whose time is their most precious resource. So getting on a call with us can be very expensive for our customers, especially with the people you really want to talk to. Having this community where they can interact with other customers and us whenever they need to on their time instead of making time for us has been super valuable. And it now even goes one step further. Our product managers and designers know that before you start emailing customers, they first need to post a question in the community. Better yet, search for your question in the community because someone has probably referenced what you're interested in. And right away, you'll find five people that want to talk to you, or you'll find the answers to your questions. For us, community has evolved the customer-centric approach to product development."

Product teams must be transparent and open in their communication to close the feedback loop after customers provide their insights. By actively being clear on which ideas, suggestions, and other feedback will make it to the roadmap and why, organizations build that trusted loop. The feedback loop is enhanced by publishing product news, new feature articles, and roadmap updates.

There are even more benefits for product teams. Product adoption will increase by articulating at scale what product and engineering teams have developed. And in the same way that communities surface a company's most loyal brand advocates, they will also surface the most engaged and helpful beta testers. Community teams have made it a standard practice to enroll their community advocates into their beta testing programs. This strengthens the beta testing program, creates an even closer bond with the advocates, and supports them in developing their knowledge and expertise. As a practical side effect, after launching the new product or feature, you already have advocates in the community that will inspire others and help other customers use these new enhancements.

And while customer communities will never entirely replace other feedback channels or remove the need for research, beta programs, and user experience testing, they do play a huge role in making the product organization more efficient, scalable, and driving stronger product adoption and satisfaction outcomes.

How Sales Teams Benefit from Community

Let's be clear—we have never come across a community program that was created, owned, or led primarily by the sales organization. Communities are places where people learn, share, and connect with others humanly and authentically. The last thing we would want to happen after joining a community is to be met with huge advertisements and continuous unsolicited sales outreach. However, that doesn't mean there isn't value for the sales organization from the community.

As we've seen, communities can help to drive customer acquisition by generating thought leadership and recommendations from loyal advocates. Rather than seeing the community as a direct lead generator, the sales team can harness community insights as part of lead tracking. Integrating the community with a CRM system such as Salesforce allows the sales team to use community data to help qualify leads. This way, organizations can track the correlation between community activity and conversion. Some organizations are starting to adopt the concept of customer success qualified leads (CSQLs) or community qualified leads (CQLs) alongside established terms like sales qualified leads (SQLs).

Also, in customer expansion (e.g., cross and upsell), a community can play a powerful role in educating customers about new or under-utilized platform functionality. Expansion opportunities with existing customers are created by demonstrating how other customers leverage certain product capabilities or by driving in-app community messaging.

So while the community is a place for authentic engagement rather than directly generating leads and sales outcomes, it does play an important role in influencing acquisition and the subsequent stages in the sales funnel.

Communication platform provider Twilio is one example where community was core to the whole go-to-market strategy. Being active in the developer ecosystem, they have benefited from community-led growth since day zero. A lot of people think of developer evangelism as a form of community, but Twilio took that one step further. People wear Twilio T-shirts; it became a brand and a symbol early on, even without Twilio even promoting it. There was so much love and interest in what Twilio was enabling that their community took a whole new form. The company was created completely bottom-up.

Talia Goldberg, partner at Bessemer Venture Partners, explains, "When Twilio went public, they even only had a few dozen sales reps. And today, they have hundreds. So obviously, the go-to-market motion has evolved as they've layered on more sales, which has been incredible and driven a lot of growth for them. Twilio's whole base and foundation is largely built on this organic and community-led movement and ecosystem. There are almost no companies that get to that scale so effectively and so efficiently. And for them, it was because of the community they built."

Conclusion

In Part I of this book, we have covered a lot of ground related to the history and evolution of communities and how leading technology companies are adopting them. Throughout the remainder of this book, we will cover everything you need to know to build a world-class community program that delivers value across your organization. In Part II, we will dive into the heart of the 10 Laws of Community— this will provide you with all the essential strategic building blocks for getting your community strategy right. And finally, in Part III, we will offer practical advice on building a thriving community program and overcoming internal hurdles.

The 10 Laws of Community Building

5

Law 1: You Can Start Anytime

It Doesn't Have to Be Expensive and Everyone in Your Organization Can Help

By Scott Salkin, Harshi Banka, and Kenneth Refsgaard

Running a business is challenging at any stage. Whether working out of your home office as you try to land and deliver for your first few customers or grappling with the challenges of scaling a global organization rallying for public market dominance, every journey has unique tests and circumstances. But nothing can compare to the diverse range of trials, tribulations, and razor-thin margins of error that come alongside those first few years of starting, funding, and scaling a new business.

Enter the power of community. For many early-stage companies, it's the benefits of being *part of* a community that help them persevere through their day-to-day challenges and decision-making. But the best startups don't only leverage communities—they make community part of their DNA from day one. That can be through local meetups, low-cost digital channels such as Medium or Slack, or even by investing in tools and resources that can help them build the foundation for more robust and meaningful interactions.

Elissa Fink, former chief marketing officer of Tableau, remembers the early days of Tableau when they had around $5 million in revenue. At that time, Tableau competed with larger traditional business intelligence (BI) platforms. She realized at the time, "If we have a happy community and they're learning and want to share, they're going to be talking about us. They'll be advocates for us, and they'll expand our awareness and our brand. They're going to amplify the power of Tableau—how great it is, how much they love it. And who's more credible talking about a product or something you know you need than someone who actually bought it and used it?"

As Fink explains, "When we lined up our first customer conference, where we really brought the early members of the community together, there were skeptics inside the company that said it was too early. They said we were not ready for community. But after that conference, people really realized internally that 'Yes, this is a thing. This is going to be something that makes us different, makes us stand out, and is going to stretch our dollars.' And it did. It created brand advocates who amplified our message."

Whether launching into a crowded market or trying to build a new category, focusing on retaining customers more efficiently, or improving product-market fit—companies are turning to their communities earlier and more often. And it doesn't have to be difficult or expensive to get started.

How to Start Tapping into Community from the Get-Go

One of the great things about the technological innovation of the past several decades is that it has provided businesses with tools and channels to engage and connect with their market more effectively, more efficiently, and more often. That said, never discount the value of meeting people in real, face-to-face settings and the additional layers of human connectedness that come with it.

And as mentioned above, it's never too early to start thinking about community. We've seen dozens of startups who have built communities *before* ever writing their first line of code or having an actual product or service to take to market. Rather than risk poor product-market fit, they invested their early time and energy in identifying and engaging with their prospective market, asking for ideas and feedback, understanding challenges and pain points, sharing concepts and prototypes, and developing rapport as a thought leader. And they're doing so not only within their own communities but also by joining others—by replying to social media posts or blog articles, by joining forums and answering community questions, or by simply attending virtual or in-person events and chatting with like-minded people. That's the beauty of community—with a little effort, you can create it practically anywhere.

The most successful companies have community built into their DNA. They're deeply focused on and committed to their relationship with their customers. From day one, they're not only thinking about how their product or service functions but how they'll leverage the power of human connection to drive the core tenets of growth—product, sales, marketing, and customer success. It's built into their mission, vision, and strategic plans. And it's a team-wide effort. A true community-driven mindset is a natural evolution from the customer experience and customer success movements of the last two decades.

So what does that mean, and how can you get started? Let's look at some of the possibilities.

Getting to Know Your Audience

Understanding your audience is something we will mention more often in this book, because it is an essential part of every phase of community-building. As you start developing your community, you need to learn about who your customers are and understand their goals, pain points, and challenges. Do they have technical questions? Are they looking to network? Are they hungry for inspiration and best practices? Are they struggling to prove value? And perhaps most importantly, how can you help them achieve their goals? As Erica Kuhl, Salesforce.com community pioneer, says, "It's extremely important to never forget that there are people behind everything that you do and to fully overemphasize what you're giving them before you expect to get anything in return. That's fundamentally how your community culture begins. If you lean heavily towards giving the community what they need, it will feel natural when you start getting value in return."

The community itself will provide you with major insights into your audience and their needs over time, but in the early stages, it can be a great practice to simply reach out to several customers and talk to them. When your audience may be initially smaller, nothing beats having direct conversations. You can also get anecdotal stories from your support and customer success organizations. Gainsight is no longer a small company, but even to this day, all senior leaders talk to numerous customers weekly. There's simply no substitute for this when it comes to understanding what's going on in their hearts and minds.

Find Your First Advocates

One of the most powerful things you can do at the beginning of any community-building effort is to start reaching the segment of your audience that is most enthusiastic about what you're doing. This will help you build an initial base of advocates who will rally around what you're creating and amplify your initiatives.

As Talia Goldberg, from Bessemer Venture Partners, explains, "You can start by targeting a small population that is passionate and interested in what you're doing. And that's great because it doesn't take many resources to do that. These people are superfans and are ecstatic when there's a platform and an ecosystem that's speaking to them.

So it starts with that, and then those people become brand ambassadors and community leaders. You can extrapolate that to most startups— it's the most effective approach."

Engage in Your Audience's Current Communities

Chances are that your customers are already actively engaged in one or several existing communities. It might be a community of practice on Slack or an independent forum. Or it could simply be a social channel such as LinkedIn, where many of us spend at least some of our time daily. Start taking small steps to directly engage where your customers are. Identify the vocal thought leaders in your field and get to know the communities they operate in. Start joining those conversations.

You can also start sharing your own perspectives in these communities, thereby directly starting to cultivate a sense of community with and between your followers. At Gainsight, the leadership team regularly shares their thoughts on LinkedIn, which has become an important part of sharing our values and ideas with the world and a way of connecting with many of our customers and industry peers. As we'll see in more detail in the next chapter, there are ultimately limits to what you can achieve when cultivating a community on borrowed ground on a social media platform in this way. Still, it is a fantastic place to start and takes minimal effort.

Start Small Initiatives to Bring Customers Together

To build a sense of community, you can start small with simple initiatives to bring customers together. In the years before its acquisition by Gainsight, inSided was a small Amsterdam-based startup with a gorgeous office in the middle of a city teeming with life and energy. In those hectic early founding years—despite being a community platform vendor since its inception—inSided didn't have its own online community. And yet, somehow, there was an extraordinary *feeling* of community with and between inSided employees and customers. What inSided did a terrific job of in those early days was community-building on a smaller scale. For example, the founding executive team invested substantial time in building human relationships with customers. Customers were regularly invited to the office for meetings, social get-togethers, and drinks. inSided's first customer was T-Mobile, and their community's superusers visited for pizza sessions and joined the inSided and T-Mobile teams on boat rides. The inSided platform's technology was immature compared to what it has become today, so the inSided team would organize innovation labs with groups of customers to share news about the roadmap, collaboratively ideate and prioritize new ideas, and simply connect and have fun. Events like this helped alleviate customers' frustrations while simultaneously closing feature gaps—and, more importantly, they created a feeling of trust and connection. One of our customers from those early years has often remarked that the culture and sense of community around the company were the "killer feature" that made inSided the obvious choice compared to competitors at that time. That particular customer, incidentally, now works for us, which says a lot in itself.

Whatever you do to facilitate this kind of community-building, the most impactful thing is that your customers will start to meet and get to know each other. We've seen time and time again that our customers love to share and learn from each other, and having been introduced, groups of our customers often initiate their own meetups and become friends over time. These experiences drive tangible long-term loyalty and advocacy, which distributes to your entire customer base.

Another example of customers meeting other customers is facilitating office hours, happy hours, or lunch-and-learn Zoom sessions. Patrick Smith, chief marketing officer at Cvent, started with these sessions during the pandemic. "We convened meetups with the community through Zoom that didn't have any agenda on the Cvent side. We weren't presenting; we were just bringing people together to vent, ask questions, and talk. We did this organically, and you had 80–100 people join because they just wanted to ask other people their perspective on industry-related things. It's amazing how just getting people together is still valuable when there's not even a topic. And even doing it virtually really got a lot of people talking, which was sometimes even therapeutic in many ways. The power of sharing ideas with others is incredibly important."

Involve Your Whole Organization in Early Efforts

When you begin to grow your community in small and simple ways, you can involve people from across your organization. Not only will this make these efforts easier to accomplish, because you will have plenty of people willing to help, but it is also a great way of deeply embedding the customer focus and community-building mindset into your organization. As you bring customers together at your office or in a virtual meetup, for example, you can invite members of your support organization that customers may have had contact with (in a support ticket) but not met in real life. Your product team can join to discuss the roadmap or feedback themes. They will better understand the people they are building the product for and will have the opportunity to receive feedback directly on their work. Your customer success team would likely be spearheading these efforts, but even if they aren't, they would likely be thrilled to play a part in initiating this kind of engagement. The founding and C-level team members can also play an important role in getting to know customers directly and making them feel appreciated and listened to.

Create Experiences That Demonstrate Your Culture and Values

In Law 10, we will be diving into culture and values in much more depth. For now, let's consider that your first community efforts are a great opportunity to start defining and sharing your culture and values with your audience. As Erica Kuhl, who built the Salesforce Trailblazer community, experienced, "It starts at the very beginning, and it's really why I think the first person that's going to be building it is the most important person to the future of the community, because they influence that culture from the very beginning." She added,

"In the early days of community-building you have this opportunity that you never have again to be very unscalable, and then to set yourself up for scale. And so all of the things you do at the very beginning are really special. And they do set that culture and that foundation and bring that personality." Whatever the first steps are that you are taking, consider that every conversation you have, meetup that you organize, and LinkedIn message that you post is laying the foundation for your long-term community culture.

Get Ready for the Next Phase of Community-Building

Throughout these early efforts, you will gain valuable insight into your customers while cultivating long-term advocacy and loyalty. This organic, unscalable community-building phase will have many magic and wonderful moments, so make the most of it and enjoy the friendships and memories you create. Because at some point, you will know it's time to enter the next phase when it becomes clear that you'll need to transition to building your community in a more scalable and sustainable way. This does not mean you must abandon the organic strategies—you can continue occasionally doing those deep dives and smaller-scale activities. But if you want to achieve business value at scale, it's time to start thinking about the next steps.

At what point is that exactly? It will be very unique for every company, of course. Still, in our experience of working with hundreds of B2B SaaS companies, you are typically ready to move into the next phase when you have gained at least 50 to 200 customers. At that point, it's no longer feasible to maintain close relationships and nurture the feeling of belonging with every individual customer using the methods we've discussed in this chapter so far. That's when you will be ready to start building your own community and investing in an owned platform. In the next chapter and throughout the remainder of this book, we will discuss how to do that.

6

Law 2: You Have to Own the Platform

Engage Your Customers Beyond Borrowed Ground

By Kenneth Refsgaard and Nadia Nicolai

As discussed in the previous chapter, community can mean many things. From simply connecting with a handful of people in a video call to organizing meetups and various other approaches, we can connect with others online. Early community-building is often based on taking steps with small groups and tapping into existing communities. These types of efforts are a great place to start and will remain relevant at every stage of maturity of your community strategy. With these efforts, you will typically engage with community members on "borrowed ground"—in other words, in a setting or on a platform you don't own. An example would be engaging with customers on a social media platform like LinkedIn or in an existing Slack, Discord, or Reddit community.

Inevitably, however, the time will come when you are ready to build and nurture your own space for customer engagement. This can include offline customer events, like Gainsight's annual Pulse conference (which we will touch on in more detail in Law 7). This book, however, will focus on building communities at scale in an "owned" online environment. In this chapter, we will explain what this means to us and why we believe this is the most effective long-term approach when creating a community for your business.

But first let's walk through the most common options that the companies we work with typically consider as they're starting to create a community program.

Building a Community on a Social Platform (Like Facebook)

A great example of "borrowed ground" is a social platform like Facebook, particularly Facebook Groups, which offers the possibility of creating a community for free and with minimal effort. This is a very tempting proposition because it requires little up-front investment and is relatively easy to experiment with. We have worked with many customers who initially started their community efforts in this way.

For community members, the barrier to entry is low: many already have the Facebook app installed on their mobile devices, the interface is familiar and intuitive, almost everyone already has an account, and the real-time notifications are already designed to drive engagement. All of this can result in a positive and low-effort experience for end users, with the potential for high engagement rates. It's no accident that 1.8 billion people use one of the 10 million available Facebook Groups every month.

So is it a good idea to start your company's community program in this way? As mentioned, it could initially be a low-effort way to start a small program and experiment. Chris Petros, chief marketing officer at ServiceTitan, says, "We've got a couple of communities, one's on Facebook, that we can't necessarily control entirely, but we moderate at some level, and then we've got our owned platform that we use on the other side of that. We've got more features and control in that owned community, and we're now starting to push people there."

There are, however, several risks and concerns that we need to consider before deciding whether using social platforms like Facebook is a viable option. As a wise man once said, 'If you're not paying for it, someone else is." In the case of Facebook and most other social platforms, as we all know, their vast revenue comes from advertisers. So we need to consider the consequences of using a platform where we (and all of our community members) essentially are the *product* instead of the customer.

At the end of the day, companies like Twitter and Facebook will chart their own course to maximize revenue from advertising, and having gained extraordinary reach and influence, they are no strangers to controversy. In the last decade, we've seen scandals involving hearings in the US Congress, user privacy violations, and ongoing issues with the spread of misinformation. Regardless of your company's integrity and values, if your customer community is built on a free advertising-based social platform like Facebook, it will be inextricably linked to any controversies tied to that platform and the direction it takes. The ultimate fate of social media platforms is also highly unpredictable, with platforms coming and going in popularity and engagement across geographies and demographics. This means that betting on one platform means accepting real risk to your program long term.

While the Facebook Groups experience includes many positive user experience elements, you have very little influence over the experience that your community members have. You can't tailor the community to the needs of your audience. A major example of this is how the content feed is automatically generated. In practice, this means that valuable content will quickly disappear from the feed, highlighting another major downside of this type of platform. It's an experience that effectively emphasizes in-the-moment engagement but conversely leads to useful content having a very short life span. The result? The same questions get asked repeatedly while useful content is continuously lost. As a community manager, you also have minimal features for moderating and monitoring content. This makes it extremely likely that you will also miss important conversations.

When working with a free social platform like Facebook, you are working on an inherently inflexible platform that isn't tailored to your business needs. You have virtually no options for customizing the features and capabilities of the community. Nor is there a transparent roadmap for the platform that you can influence. Functionality can and will change with little notice.

Another major concern with platforms like Facebook Groups is that you do not have access to all of the content and data from the community. Some basic metrics might be available but will be constrained and largely ineffective for the community insights needed for advanced community programs to optimize engagement and prove business value. Therefore, reviewing and curating valuable content effectively is also largely impossible.

The final factor that we will consider is that with a Facebook Group, you are effectively creating a siloed destination that is disconnected from the rest of your customers' digital journey. You can, of course, include some cross-linking and promotion, but the community will very much live separately from your other touchpoints. You won't be able to elegantly integrate the experience with other touchpoints. Search engines won't crawl the community's content, so the content will remain findable only to those who actively visit the community.

There's plenty more that we could say on this topic, but the above themes should already paint a picture of why we don't generally recommend starting a serious community program on a platform like Facebook Groups.

Eurail is an example of a company that transitioned away from Facebook Groups, despite having a very active group. As Nanja Schalkwijk, the Eurail community manager, told us, "As Facebook is mainly catered to showing the most recent information, our community needed a dedicated branded community platform for our members to support each other with information and inspiration in a more efficient and effective way. It also allowed us to own our data, to sustain our community in the long term, and for all information to be found easily within the platform as well as outside of it."

Building a Community on a Collaboration Platform (like Slack)

Slack has become the standard-bearer for internal collaboration in technology companies, and the user experience is now a trusted and familiar part of the day-to-day lives of millions of people. We increasingly hear questions from companies about whether a Slack (or Discord) community is a good idea and if it can be part of a broader ecosystem that includes an owned on-domain community. Some companies may even consider making Slack the centerpiece of their entire community program.

The power of the Slack experience lies in driving (close to) real-time collaboration and engagement. It is a fantastic place to ask a quick question or take part in an ongoing conversation. The taxonomy of Slack channels is usually formed around groups of employees working together, which has helped to drive a revolution in the possibilities for collaboration and the sense of belonging within remote or globally dispersed teams.

So is it possible to open up a community in Slack and make that the centerpiece of a community program? Yes, it is, and we've seen powerful examples of this structure. In the world of community practitioners, the CMX Slack community is a great place to connect with other industry professionals. If the focus is going to be on driving high levels of activity and fostering a sense of belonging, then Slack is also a great option.

However, when it comes to building a community for your customers, there are some important limitations that are worth considering.

A major one is the fact that content in Slack is unstructured. Conversations in Slack happen within channels that are typically centered around a particular theme. Within a single channel, the conversation will be an endless stream of discussion, often jumping between many different topics. It's possible to follow this unstructured flow if you are reading all new posts on a daily basis—as may be the case if you're using it as an internal collaboration tool for your team. But when customers browse a new channel or look for something specific at a given time, they will most likely be lost. Similar to Facebook Groups, content is "buried" quickly. This means helpful content doesn't get the reach it deserves, and community members are likely to ask the same questions repeatedly.

Like Facebook Groups, a Slack community also has limited options to customize the experience for your audience. Some level of organization is possible, thanks to the functionality of channels and other useful native features. That said, you're largely working with the default interface of Slack with limited possibilities to optimize the experience—for instance, there's no ability to highlight valuable content or integrate the community experience with other digital touchpoints.

Finally, with Slack, you also lock away all your content in a silo. While Slack does allow you to build smart technical integrations, there is one major downside to a platform like this that you can't integrate your way out of: search engines do not crawl the content. There is simply no possibility of benefiting from long-tail content in a Slack community. This means that you will be "losing" tons of useful content and, similar to Facebook Groups, inevitably find that the same questions and topics are raised over and over again.

As we have covered above, there are good reasons not to create your customer community solely on Slack. However, as we have also mentioned, we don't want to dismiss the power of this platform in terms of delivering fantastic (near) real-time engagement. It's absolutely possible to consider having a Slack community as part of a broader engagement ecosystem where it serves a distinct purpose different from the centrally owned community. And due to a myriad of Slack integrations, you can easily surface community content within Slack channels using (potentially Zapier-powered) integration.

The Power of an Owned Platform

So far we've considered two technology options for creating a community program, both of which have raised concerns that would make us hesitant to recommend them as the heart of a community program. These "borrowed ground" platforms are different from an "owned platform." But what, exactly, does this mean?

Owning a platform does not mean building and hosting your own platform. While doing this is theoretically possible, and there are a handful of technology companies with the appetite to do so, most companies opt to select an enterprise SaaS platform for their community program versus building something from scratch. The reason is simple: the total cost of ownership when building, hosting, and maintaining it yourself will inevitably exceed that of a SaaS platform. And a great SaaS platform is likely to be far superior to what you could realistically achieve on your own when it comes to features, security, and long-term stability. These are all the same reasons that most companies don't attempt to build and host their own CRM platform.

Many options are available in the SaaS space, so let's continue defining what we mean by "owned platform" by breaking down the main capabilities that we believe are essential in a next-generation customer community program.

- **It's a seamless part of your online ecosystem.** The fragmentation of touchpoints—as we will cover in much greater detail in Chapter 8—is a major challenge for many B2B SaaS companies. The last thing we want to do when creating a community program is to create another fractured and siloed experience. Instead, we believe it's important for the community to become a seamless part of the online experience. In practice, this typically means that it shares the same web (sub) domain as the main website, has a consistent design and user experience, and is fully integrated across the website and product. As the community grows and starts to pull in traffic via search engines, an additional benefit is that traffic will flow to other parts of the site, such as the marketing or product pages.

■ **You can personalize the experience for your audience.**
Every company, product, and audience is unique, so it's important to be able to customize and personalize the experience for
your unique situation. For example, it's incredibly valuable to
be able to optimize the layouts of your community pages to
reflect the stage of the individual customer life cycle. Having
the flexibility to highlight specific content that is recent and
engaging, or even better, to be able to automatically surface
content that is relevant to a visitor or segment of members, is
going to radically improve the engagement rates in the community. In fact, an owned platform will offer you nearly limit-
less options to fine-tune the experience based on customer
health, customer journey or life cycle stages, or other account
data available in your customer success or CRM system.

■ **Content is structured and findable.** In Chapter 3 we covered the historical roots of communities in the bulletin boards
and forums of the 1990s and how they have evolved alongside
other social and engagement platforms. An owned community
platform will generally share a few notable elements with traditional "forums"—namely the fact that content is structured and
easy to find. In contrast to the endlessly scrolling channels in a
platform like Slack or the content that disappears after it's been
seen once in your Facebook feed and never to be seen again,
content is typically created as "topics" or "articles" with clear
subject lines and opening posts that outline what the piece of
content and subsequent discussion is about. Below that there
may be many replies. The extraordinary power of this way of
structuring content lies in the possibility for other community
members being able to effectively search for, find, follow, and
read discussions that are relevant to them. This enhanced findability means that useful content will tend to have a very "long
tail" and may be read by thousands of other readers over a long
period of time. Combined with the fact that most owned communities are at least partly open to be crawled by search (or AI!)
engines, this results in the owned community platform acting as

a content creation powerhouse and becoming an extraordinary repository of inspiring and helpful content.

- **Content types are rich and engaging.** There are many capabilities that you will only get with an owned community platform, an important one being the opportunity to go far beyond the simple and uniform text-based content types that you find in other platforms—for example, the possibility to have a section of "ideas" that community members can vote on, or to create "events" that highlight virtual or in-person engagement moments. You could create "articles" for your most engaging company-created content or "product updates" that highlight new features and releases. All in all, it means a lot more flexibility in creating an experience that is fine-tuned to the needs of your audience, which platforms like Slack cannot offer.

- **You have access to all data and content.** In contrast to the other options we have considered so far, with an owned platform you also have unlimited access to all the data and content. Having access to deep data and insights into your community program will allow you to understand and optimize the performance of your community as well as allow you to measure business value (which we will cover in detail in Law 9). You will also have unlimited options for making the most of all the content in your community because you *own* the data.

- **You can integrate it with your technology stack.** Finally, an owned community platform will give you numerous options to make the platform a seamless part of your technology stack. This might mean integrating with your CRM (e.g., Salesforce), customer success (e.g., Gainsight), and BI (e.g., Tableau) platforms so that you have an accurate 360-degree view of your customers and their community activity. It also might mean elegantly integrating with your ticketing and help desk system (e.g., Zendesk) to power federated search and ticket escalation from the community. And with APIs and modern low-code tools like Zapier, you can easily create custom integrations. This will ensure that your community program delivers a seamless experience for both customers and employees rather than becoming another data and content silo.

Mary Poppen, customer intelligence strategist and board advisor at Involve.ai and author of *Goodbye, Churn. Hello, Growth!*, realized these challenges. According to Poppen, "You can do communities on LinkedIn. You could have a Facebook page, an Instagram page or Twitter page. Yes, you can get a community built with those tools as well, but you need to manage them and it's very siloed. So how do you centralize and bring all of that together? It's really challenging. I think an owned community platform is the springboard. It's a centralized location for all of the thought leadership, ideas, knowledge and product information, to flow to and from. For example, our customer learning platform is fully integrated with the community, with an amazing seamless customer experience. We were able to streamline and track everything through a centralized community platform. So for me, I think a platform is necessary to really build a strategic community strategy, not to overuse the word strategy. But without it, I think it's very hard to manage, and you get very siloed information. And I think the customer experience is choppier that way as well."

Summary

So far, we've covered how to start your early community-building initiatives in many (initially small) ways. We've also argued that ultimately, in order to build a scalable and effective community program for your customers, you will want to implement an online community platform. As we've seen, there are many benefits to owning the platform compared to the most common alternatives. By selecting an enterprise-grade owned community platform, you will truly be able to own the experience and create and offer something to your customers that is deeply optimized for them. In the next chapter, we will look at how your platform strategy can connect to your customers' journey.

7

Law 3: Community Should Be the Heart of the Customer Journey

Activate and Engage Your Customers at Scale

By Aaron Hatton and Haiko Krumm

In the previous chapters, we have seen how communities can contribute to your organization and that you need to start early with your community efforts. We also learned that the most valuable way to implement an online community is to own the platform. In this chapter, we want to build on that and explain how community is at the heart of any customer journey.

By "at the heart of the customer journey," we mean delivering valuable content and engagement to the customer at the right time and place. Your community is the strategic platform that centralizes all content and engagement relevant to end users in one single destination. But that doesn't mean you want to move customers toward the community as a destination by itself, with a separate customer journey. Instead, centralized content should be carefully and strategically intertwined with your pre-existing customer journey to help elevate your customer experience. Rather than living alone and in a silo, your community should be embedded with your product or service throughout multiple locations, especially areas where a customer may need additional guidance or support. But before we dive into community and the customer journey, let's first review what a customer journey is.

Customer Life Cycle and Customer Journey Explained

With every customer, their relationship with your organization is often referred to as a journey. Whether it's a customer who has stuck by you for the past 10 years or a customer who just signed up, that journey differs depending on the stage in your relationship.

Because a community is a vital part of your long-term strategy and not just a one-time marketing campaign, the community can continue to play a longer-term role in the journey your customers experience with your company over time. It can help customers grow and flourish on their own or can be used to accelerate the growth of passionate and engaged customers.

The concept of the customer journey comes in many different definitions, shapes, and forms. In an ideal world, the customer journey covers both the pre-sales and post-sales phases, because it should be one smooth experience for the customer.

There is also a key difference between the customer life cycle and the customer journey. Customer life cycle and customer journey are terms often mistakenly thought to be the same thing. The customer life cycle is the entire process of managing a customer. It describes the various stages a customer goes through before, during, and after they buy your products or service. As Claudia Imhoff and colleagues (2000) wrote:

> The purpose of the customer life cycle is to define and communicate the stages through which a customer progresses when considering, purchasing and using products, and the associated business processes a company uses to move the customer through the customer life cycle.

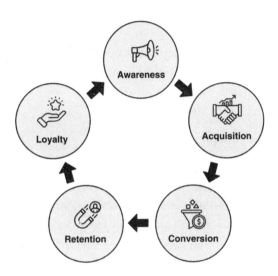

The customer life cycle tracks business performance over time by measuring results in each stage. It has an *inside-out* focus. The life cycle can be visualized as a circle, timeline, funnel, bow tie, or infinity loop. For the purpose of this book, we'll keep it simple and show it as a circle. The life cycle is usually defined in five to eight different stages with different names. In B2B environments, it generally comes down to these five steps.

1. **Awareness** (also called "reach" or "discovery") is the first stage of the life cycle, where your customers (prospects) realize they have a problem they want to solve. In this stage, you want your customers to become aware of your solution and your brand.

2. **Acquisition** is the stage where you are on a prospect's radar, and you'll want to start engaging with them to convert them into a lead. This stage is all about turning a prospect aware of your brand or product into a potential buyer.

3. **Conversion** is the stage of the life cycle where you convert the prospect and sell the product. This is the most visible stage of the pre-sales phase, where usually most of the effort of the sales team is going.

4. **Retention** stage starts once the initial sales are finalized, and at this point your new customers are typically handed over to your customer success teams.

5. **Loyalty** is the final stage, and in a perfect world, every single customer you acquire would make it to this stage. At this point, the customer is not only satisfied with your product but also enthusiastic about advocating for it.

With the stages defined, let's take a moment to delve a little deeper into the retention phase. As we explained in our first book, *Customer Success, How Innovative Companies Are Reducing Churn and Growing Recurring Revenue,* the retention stage is crucial for SaaS companies. It's where the promises and expectations from the first three stages have to be translated into perceived experience and value. The customer life cycle clearly stems from the transactional economy, with more "pre-sales" than "post-sales" stages, whereas for SaaS—in the subscription economy—the post-sales phase should be longer than the pre-sales phase to create a sustainable business. Therefore the retention stage is divided into the substages of **onboarding, adoption, nurturing,** and **renewal/growth.** We'll dive more deeply into these substages when we explore how the community is at the heart of the customer journey.

Journey Map to Define the Desired Customer Journey

As mentioned earlier, the customer life cycle is an "inside-out" description of the steps the company would like its customers to go through. A customer journey, however, describes the path of sequential steps and interactions that a customer takes with a company, product, or service. It is "outside-in" and much less straightforward and predictable. In fact, we dare to say that every customer's journey is unique. Even if you have an online-only company with only one website and standardized emails, the experience every customer has will be different. They find your website via different paths, have different backgrounds and expectations, are in different locations and times, and have different distractions and surroundings. And in B2B, who are we actually referring to as the customer? Is it the company? Is it an individual employee within the company?

To deal with this challenge, we create a journey map. It is a visualization of the predetermined, desired path for a customer to go through. The journey map connects the "outside-in" customer experience with the "inside-out" customer life cycle. It is a proven method invented in 1985 by Chip Bell and Ron Zemke. They created the first journey map for a giant telephone company receiving more complaint calls from customers than usual and wanted to understand the causes and solutions for the change. This was when all telephones either sat on a table or were mounted on a wall, and long before monitoring products like Gainsight PX or Datadog.

Most companies will have different journey maps for different customer segments. For each journey map, you define the customer life cycle stages you want to cover. Within the journey map, you take different personas into account—for instance, Sarah, the CCO and decision-maker; Paul, the administrator; Claire, the superuser; and Kyle, the end user. The journey map should emphasize the key milestones and "moments of truth," those select interactions when customers invest much emotional energy in important outcomes, the AHA moments where they say, "Now I see why I invested in your product and put trust in your business," And last but not least, a journey map is not set in stone. It should be continuously tracked and optimized.

Community at the Heart of the Customer Journey

Now that we have explained the customer life cycle, the customer journey, and the journey map, it's time to dive into the role of community within the customer journey.

Throughout the multiple stages of the customer journey, a community not only can improve the customer's experience but can elevate it without the need for individual intervention from your organization's teams.

However, to be clear, simply having a customer community won't win you the multimillion-dollar tender. It won't ensure your customer renews with you every year. It won't avoid every customer risk. What it can do, however, if leveraged correctly, is elevate the customer experience and provide customers with a meaningful resource, thereby ensuring they get value out of your product and will keep investing in your partnership. And a community can do so at scale and without needing one-to-one interaction.

Community as a Concept versus Content and Engagement Within

Before we delve deeper, it's essential to first understand the difference between integrating the community as a concept into your customer journey versus integrating community content and engagement. When we refer to the concept of a community, we're not discussing the definition as we have done in previous chapters, but more so how to attract members and activate the community. This can be valuable and necessary to grow the community and give the customer insights and belonging in the long term. But this doesn't bring immediate value to your customer.

As we explained earlier, you create a journey map to define the desired path for a customer to go through. During the onboarding phase, for instance, you want your customers to get the product up and running, and you want them to learn about the product. While it would be great if they become an active community member simultaneously, that's not the main objective of this stage and shouldn't be the main objective of getting the community at the heart of your customer journey.

Let's walk through an example to make it clear. Say you are a sales leader, and you've just bought a new CRM tool. You receive a welcome email saying, "We have a great community with over 2,000 members where you can find a lot of information about our product. Sign up today." That email promotes the community as a concept. On the other hand, the email could say, "Here are the five things to decide before setting up your CRM tool to ensure long-term success," or perhaps, "Read how other companies use our dashboard during their weekly sales meeting to increase funnel conversion." This email promotes community content and engagement. Hopefully, this clarifies that promoting community content and engagement brings more immediate value than promoting the community as a concept. When done well, it probably would lead to even more community activation than when you promote the community as a concept.

When bringing the community to the heart of the customer journey, the starting point should always be, "What's in it for the customer? What is the value add that you are trying to provide for your customers? How does this impact their experience throughout their customer journey?" These questions should help influence the design and architecture of your community and any content creation you plan for. The use cases for integrating community content and engagement differ across the different stages of the customer journey.

Nevertheless, it should also be clear that you should not create separate community journeys and personas compared to what you already use in your existing organization and already defined by the marketing team. We've seen many community teams create a separate set of personas, but the community shouldn't be treated as a silo that targets different users or purposes versus the rest of your organization.

Stages of the Customer Journey, from Onboarding to Pre-Sales

As we mentioned, the customer life cycle can be broken down in a few different ways. For the purposes of this book, we've broken it down into five stages: awareness, acquisition, conversion, retention, and loyalty. And we've further split up the retention stage into onboarding, adoption, nurturing, renewal, and growth.

As a customer community initially focuses on existing customers, we also start by diving into the post-sales phases and only at the end explain how the community contributes to the pre-sales phases.

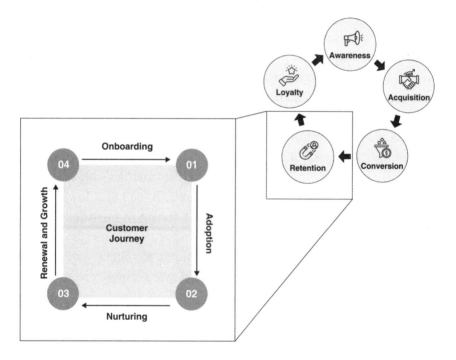

Onboarding

A customer enters the onboarding phase once the "dotted line" is signed and all the contractual paperwork has been completed. The customer onboarding phase is probably the most important post-sales phase and sets the tone for the rest of the journey. There is excitement and energy within your customer's organization to start using your product. Customers can also be anxious to get started, because there are a lot of unknowns ahead and extra work during the onboarding phase. In this stage, you want to show your customers that they are in good hands and activate them, helping set everything up correctly and ensuring they learn what they need to know about your product.

During onboarding, your customer looks to integrate your product into their way of working and often even technically with other tools and data sources. As your customers begin this process, your community can be used as the reference point for how to complete some of the more technical parts of the initial setup and configuration. With the community guides written and shared, if your customer has additional questions, they can take advantage of your comment section, creating a learning loop that will not only help other customers but help your community team keep optimizing and adding content. For example, at Gainsight, we posted an article in our community using Zapier integrations. You can easily find this article when you are working on the integration from within the Gainsight admin environment, and consequently the article has been read almost 2,000 times. In response to the article, customers asked how to integrate with Asana via Zapier, how to get API keys, and many other relevant questions. They received their answers, and the article has since been updated to include additional information, helping answer their questions for future readers.

The power of discussion via the community during the onboarding phase can be incredible. Encouraging recently onboarded customers to sign up and participate in roundtable discussions with others can also help to bring forward common challenges and struggles, allowing your teams to understand the key areas to focus resources on and help better support your customers. After all, all your customers combined likely know more about your product and how to use it than you do.

Delivering community content throughout the onboarding phase can be done in many different ways. You can bring the content to your customers with an initial onboarding email, welcoming them to your product and inviting them to explore resources in your community. You may also find it helpful to provide onboarding tips using in-app checklists or popups with links back to the community content throughout multiple points of your product or service. This will not only provide affirmation that it is a vital resource, but it also helps customers get the right information they need from the community when they need it, without the need to reach out to a member of your team.

Adoption

The next step of progression during the onboarding phase is the adoption stage. Customers need to start *using* your product, making it part of their everyday routine. Throughout this phase, your customers will want to feel reassured and supported, while the experience is typically less intensive than what they had experienced throughout the onboarding phase.

At this stage, promoting the community as a concept can be valuable. You can share a gentle statement of the benefits of joining the community. Making customers feel welcome, keeping up the momentum, and encouraging them to engage with events such as roundtables or networking meetups in your customer community can be a great way to begin getting involved.

Throughout this phase, there may also be times when customers don't know what features of functionality they should or could be using. Perhaps they've had a new change of direction, or even expanded their deployment to include additional scope. By leveraging existing data points from your product or service analytic tools, you can understand their depth and breadth of adoption when using your product or service and then use this data to create tailored messaging toward relevant community content and events. Not only does this provide customers with the right guidance when needed, but it also ensures that your product/service is working to make their lives easier. For example, suppose a customer hasn't yet adopted your mobile app. In that case, sending them an email explaining the benefits, with a community discussion, case study, and how-to guide, will provide quantifiable results quickly as they realize the value and increase their return on investment.

Perhaps there may even be a use case for a setting or configuration option within your product or service, which is commonly overlooked. It's a feature or functionality from which your customer can derive great value, but it is often something that your customer success and support teams need to guide your customers through how to use it. By leveraging in-app messaging and email notifications, you could create a tailored message for your customer, linking to a community post or case study informing them about the benefits of making the change and how to do so.

Nurturing

After some time, customers will meet several milestones with your product, whether that is a number of documents created, interactions with a feature or tool, or a number of transactions completed. Once they reach this point, they are typically referred to as having entered the nurturing stage. This is seen as your "business as usual." You will most commonly find your longer-standing customers within this phase, as they know your product or service well—and for the most part, everything should, at this point, be second nature.

Customers in the nurturing stage typically have challenges at a few common points in their journey:

1. They need to go over a tactical issue.
2. Your point of contact has left, and a new user, admin, or decision-maker takes over.
3. Something in your product or service has changed.
4. Their needs or requirements have changed.

These challenges can be easily tackled by leveraging the power of a great community.

Let's start with the first of the four challenges. It's not uncommon to have a productive call with a customer on a Friday afternoon, and by Monday morning, you and your customer have forgotten not only what you have spoken about but also what is needed to complete a specific action or ask for your product or service. Sending a follow-up email after your call with links to written guides or tutorials hosted on your customer community is a great way to share resources, drive foot traffic, and keep the conversation going. Customers can leave a comment on the guide/tutorial asking a question, and before you return to work on Monday morning, you may find it is answered by another customer who had a similar challenge.

For customers employing digital-led strategies in particular, your community can provide a scalable channel with a personal touch. Customers can search their questions, and if you have integrated your community well, they can do so directly from within your product. Otherwise, they can find it through your support page or knowledge base. With federated search, you can ensure that customers can find all the relevant content from different sources within one search. For instance, Unqork, a company that provides a no-code application platform, integrated the community federated search with their learning management system (LMS), content management system (CMS), and marketplace. As we mentioned earlier, even if they don't know where to go and use Google for their question, they often find their answer in the community.

Did you know an average of 30% to 70% of all community traffic comes via Google? In the community, they can also ask questions directly or add follow-up questions on existing content.

A similar approach can be helpful if your main point of contact has left your customers' organization. As you complete your initial introductions, you can invite your new point of contact to join your other customers in roundtables and community discussions. This helps them to feel like they are part of your existing community, get their foot in the door, and learn how other organizations benefit from your product or services. This method has been proven to be very effective time and time again for organizations of all sizes. You can also use the flow we mentioned in the onboarding and adoption phases for new users using your product. Because you will have the date of when the customer (i.e., the company) was onboarded and when the user (i.e., your new point of contact) was onboarded, you can create a customized path providing resources and linking the roundtables and community discussions.

It's not only the changes for the customer for which the community may be useful in guiding—after all, we as humans struggle with change. So whenever something changes, it can be difficult for us to adapt and continue working the way we were before or even adjust to the new way of doing things. To help overcome these challenges, many books and subject specialties focus specifically on change management and how best to adapt to overcome this challenge, but for the purpose of this book, let's narrow our focus on how a community can help.

Whenever a part of your product or service is updated or changed, you should make a point to post about it in your community in advance. Not only will this help you get ahead of the change management process, but you can also use it as a point of reference once the changes have occurred. For example, let's say you move a commonly used "New project" button from one menu to another. When the menu is displayed, you can show a tool tip asking your customer, "Are you looking to create a new project? This has now moved to . . ." and "Learn more about this change here." That way, you are not only informing the customer of the change, but you are also providing them with the reasoning behind the change and the potential opportunity to discuss the changes with other customers and your product team through the power of community. By providing a periodical product update article, your customers can get excited by change, inspired to try new things, and see the continuous optimization your product and development team brings them.

Finally, the hardest challenge is if a customer's needs or requirements have changed. Typically, this is something you come to discover as part of a conversation, whether that's part of a regular meeting or the customer is reaching out asking to schedule a call. By this point you're on the defensive, if you will, trying to turn the conversation around from not needing your product or service to how your product and service can be used differently to meet their new needs.

While conversing with your customer, you may find that the best approach is to tell a story. This way, your customers feel as though you've not only heard their new needs or requirements but you've faced similar challenges with different clients and can bring that experience to the table. A great way to showcase this is by creating case studies with existing customers and sharing these with your customer community. This allows other customers to join in on the conversation. Perhaps they are about to face a similar challenge, and it is a similar scenario. If not, then it becomes a great reference point for you to share with that customer we mentioned earlier.

Throughout the process of tackling all of these challenges, several methods are available to you that can help drive traffic to your community and help your customers preemptively. As we discussed, it's all about providing the right information at the right time. For example, if you find that typically a number of your customers ask for benchmark data on how they should leverage your products or services at specific times of the year, why not provide this information in advance? Linking customers back to the community, which hosts the monthly, quarterly, biannual, or annual benchmarking, can be a great way to start a conversation.

A great example of a consumer business that does this is Spotify. At the end of every year, they provide a "Year in Review" with stats on which artists you've listened to the most, your top songs, and music genres. This coincidently works as a great marketing strategy because they also provide a way for everyone to share the results of their year via social media. Providing a similar experience for B2B may not be as exciting or something customers will share on their Facebook accounts. Still, it could be something that your customer champion presents at their next board meeting to help justify the value of your products or services.

Keeping on track with the automated experiences, several additional avenues could be explored from an automated perspective during the nurturing phase to help promote the use of the customer community. One suggestion would be if a customer's idea request were to be included in the next release. Creating a notification from the list of customers who created similar ideas, and upvoted/commented, can be a great way to show customers how the community is actually providing value.

Renewal / Growth

In the final stage of our customer journey, we have renewal and growth. This stage can be strange at times because it has several different "wild card" elements to it. For example, as part of the growth phase, you may need your customer to reenter the onboarding phase. Alternatively, as part of the renewal phase, your customer may no longer be part of your customer journey. With a great community supporting your team, you can reduce friction and improve your customer experience.

One great example of this is when pitching a growth opportunity. This could be part of a midterm expansion or even their end-of-contract renewal. As you have these discussions with your end customer, customers typically ask, "How is this product/service/feature benefiting other customers like us?" You can provide a link not only to case studies typically hosted on your website but access to your customer community where they can ask and read about existing customers' experiences.

These same conversations can also be useful for customers with feature requests on the upcoming roadmap or may be popular in your customer community. Linking customers to the customer community shows the demand for particular features, the weight it carries, and that your product teams are engaged and actively reviewing the feedback from the customer community. In turn, this will not only drive more use of your community, but it will also help build a level of trust and rapport with your customers, helping them feel reassured that if they ever need to make a feature request, they are in safe hands. What do you think happens when your customers see their requested feature being delivered and a product manager thanking them for their great feedback? Chances are high that they will be very happy and enter the loyalty phase.

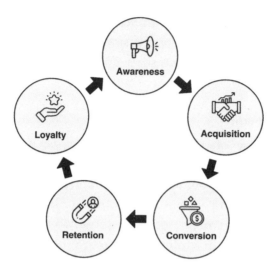

Loyalty

Now we've covered the four substages of retention, let's take a moment to step into the next stage of the customer life cycle: loyalty. Loyalty and community go hand-in-hand, because your superusers in your community will also be your most loyal customers. After all, why would you put so much effort into a community if you don't like the product or company? You could do so in the short term, but generally people who don't like your product (detractors) won't take a very active role in the community, unless they *truly care* about helping improve your product or service.

The loyalty phase is where the fun really starts. Everyone knows the net promoter score (NPS) question: "How likely are you to recommend this company or product to a friend or colleague?" This is a theoretical question showing likelihood, not showing actions. Well, in a community it's put into action. Your superusers are promoting your company and your product on a regular basis, sometimes even daily. Every post will show their engagement and expertise, with most superusers often posting as much as 20% of all community content. It's a flywheel for positive community engagement. Yes, they also will be critical occasionally, but if handled correctly, that only increases the sense of community, just like a relationship with a friend grows stronger when you've had some friction that is resolved.

To attract and grow your superusers, you often build specific programs. Veeam, for instance, is a company with a powerful program called Veeam Legends. Ksenia Zvereva and Rick Vanover spearheaded the creation of this program. As they explain in their community:

> Veeam Legends are Veeam users and data protection industry experts who are passionate about technology, innovation and eager to further develop their career, while sharing their experiences with the community. As avid Veeam users, they participate in various community projects, drive local Veeam User Groups, and can also influence development of Veeam products and solutions— they have real impact within the community! Apart from that, Veeam Legends are always eager to help their peers and get connected with other community members.

You can only become a Veeam Legend by invitation. To be invited, you have to show valuable participation within their community, which is rewarded with points and badges.

When you become a Veeam Legend, you get access to a private group, special beta programs, direct interaction with the product team, and some swag. Also worthy of mention: Veeam has a great weekly community recap. It's a 10- to 30-minute video update in which the community team highlights valuable events and content and thanks their contributors. At the time of writing, they have already posted over 100 community recaps, and every single one gets many views and comments.

Pre-Sales

Once you have built your community with the post-sales phases in mind, it's great to take a moment to step back and think about how it can also impact your pre-sales phase. Community is often seen only as a selling point during the pre-sales phase—something go-to-market teams will talk with customers about and promote as a unique value proposition to help improve their customer experience. However, if leveraged correctly, it can be much more than that.

Your community will provide you and your customers (and prospects) with value through every pre-sales cycle, from awareness to acquisition and conversion. Beginning the process of creating awareness can be challenging. Most existing customers find your community content via a Google search, links, and snippets on external media like LinkedIn. This will bring your brand and solution to them at the right moment and with the "approved by our customer community" stamp on it.

As your sales teams are talking with prospective customers, your community should be pitched as a means to showcase recent feature releases and customer case studies and provide evidence of existing customers actively engaged in both conversations, use case sharing, and feature requests.

There is a great deal of content that can be valuable throughout the pre-sales stage. This content also provides excellent value throughout other stages of the customer journey. Sharing customer case studies on your community is a great way to promote the community, create visibility, and encourage visitors to register. It also allows for your community to become the source of truth, allowing customers and prospects alike to discuss the case studies in the comment section and ask questions.

There's also the added benefit of leveraging integration how-to guides, which would typically be used later, such as onboarding being leveraged in this pre-sales stage. Most prospective customers will typically request more information about the integrations available and the ability to share technical documentation. It allows their technical or development teams to review and confirm that it meets their expectations before making any commitments and meeting with your technical sales teams.

And of course, we can't forget feature requests—a great way to show the organic growth of your product through direct customer feedback as features move from ideation to work in progress and then completed. If your prospect has a feature request during the conversations, it can also be a great place to encourage them to post it and get the ball rolling on getting other existing customers to voice their support.

It Starts with Valuable Content

As discussed at the start of this chapter, "Community at the heart of the customer journey" means delivering valuable content and engagement to the customer at the right time and place. We've explained why you should integrate the community into your customer journey and shared some ideas on how to do that. The table on page 94 summarizes some of those ideas.

But how do you create valuable content? That's what the next chapter is all about.

	Onboarding	Adoption	Nurturing	Renewal/Growth	Loyalty	Pre-Sales
Objective	Show initial value by implementing the product and training the customer	Become an integral part of the customer's daily activities and operations	Continue "business as usual"	Keep and grow customers	Turn customers into advocates that share success stories	Use content and advocacy to convert new customers
Community integration	Integration articles Content for tips and tricks emails New customer user groups and training	Customer roundtables Customer use cases Highlight underused features & functionalities Product feedback	Self-help content Q&A Product updates New user training Customer case studies and benchmarks	Case studies Feature requests Roadmap updates Customer challenge discussions	Superuser programs Loyalty programs Private groups Beta programs	Case studies References Meetups Reviews Content that increases knowledge and trust with prospects

8 | Law 4: Create Content That Educates and Inspires

Be the Best Thought Leader You Can Be

By Remco de Vries and Kenneth Refsgaard

In the last chapter, we discussed how important your community can be throughout the customer journey. For that to happen, there is one vital ingredient that you simply must have, and that's content. An active and engaged community will undoubtedly create a large volume of user-generated content as members ask questions, connect, and share knowledge with each other. But there's a significant opportunity and role for you to play in content creation as well.

As discussed, a community is a group of people coming together with a common purpose. If you create and facilitate a space for them, they will naturally form relationships and interact as a group.

The content you provide, however, can help steer that process, to facilitate connections and guide the community toward the results and outcomes you want.

Therefore, your content strategy will broadly be defined by the use cases you focus on for your community. When you prioritize delivering self-service, you will require a specific approach to content, just like how establishing thought leadership within your category will need another distinct flavor of content.

Particularly in the early growth phases, your content will clarify and communicate your community's intended use cases to its members. It's a way to ensure that there is something for community members to look at and to start discussing from the moment they join.

At Gainsight, we sometimes illustrate content's role with this simple flywheel. Content will initially help drive traffic to your community. From that traffic, you will see community activation in the form of engagement, which results in more content creation, and so on. This ongoing cycle is a simple and helpful way to illustrate how successful communities grow.

As this is a broad and important topic, let's dive deeper into what we mean by community content and the different purposes and types of content that exist.

The Four Pillars of Community Content

When developing a community content strategy, we recommend considering the various objectives and goals that your content can serve. This will help develop an effective strategy where it's clear what value every piece of content is meant to deliver and how that maps to your business goals. Below is a simple model outlining four critical pillars of community content that we recommend considering.

Content Pillar	Description
Help	The self-service use case is foundational for many digital-led customer success communities. Thus it's natural that service-focused content is one of the key pillars of many community content strategies. Help content is focused on helping customers solve problems. Specific content themes are often sourced from the support teams or from frequently occurring questions. They are intended to answer the most common or the most straightforward questions, freeing up the customer-facing teams to focus on more value-add interactions. *Impacting metrics: Increased self-service and support ticket reduction*
Educate	With the rise of B2B SaaS, many communities have shifted focus toward creating content that is primarily focused on supporting the activities of the customer success team. This means educational content specifically aimed at helping customers get value from the product, typically via how-to guides, examples, and best practices. Other possibilities here are product functionality updates and content highlighting particular product capabilities to drive adoption. This is, of course, customer success at scale—or digital customer success, one of the hottest topics in the CS world as we write this book. *Impacting metrics: Reduced churn and increased product adoption*

(continued)

(*continued*)

Content Pillar	Description
Engage	When establishing a felt sense of community there is a need for content directly aimed at driving engagement. This might be content about the community, for example, highlighting and summarizing recently discussed subjects or spotlighting individual members. There can also be room for fun and irreverent content like jokes, contests, and quizzes. This will often be content aimed at starting conversations to invite deeper discussion and facilitate networking between customers. ***Impacting metrics:*** *Monthly active customers*
Inspire	Inspirational content is intended to establish thought leadership around your category, brand, and product. Developing your position as a thought leader will be essential in establishing advocacy among customers and extending a sense of community to noncustomers interested in your space. Consider, for example, how Gainsight is seen as a customer success thought leader and how Gainsight's thought leadership has become influential and respected across the customer success space. Ultimately, this can be a crucial driver of new business. ***Impacting metrics:*** *Retention and growth*

Where to Focus Your Attention

As we've seen above, there are a few possible flavors of community content, and you might consider investing in all of them. But if you're looking to focus and prioritize, we recommend investing primarily in content that is *educational and inspirational*. The reason is simple. We believe that for community content to be effective from a business perspective, it needs to be relevant and valuable—and most members join a company's community because they want to learn. For this reason, educational and inspirational content is at the heart of communities built by B2B SaaS companies.

Just think about the last business webinar you joined. You probably signed up for it because the subject was closely related to your profession, and you expected to pick up useful learnings. Our lives are busy, and there is a staggering amount of content in the world for us to consume. Therefore, we naturally segment our time and filter what gets our attention. For community content to be effective, it must genuinely educate us about an important topic.

So how to define educational and inspirational content? To answer this question, we need to peel back the layers of why someone joins your community. For most communities, it will be for one of the following reasons:

- They have taken an interest in your company, brand, product, or service and are looking to learn more.
- They have bought your product or service and are looking to optimize their usage by asking questions and learning best practices.
- They want to meet and network with peers in a similar situation (and possibly industry).
- They are experts in your product or service and want to develop their careers by deepening their expertise and positioning themselves as thought leaders.

In each of these cases, it will mostly be your educational and inspirational content that will serve the needs of your members. Your content will educate about your product or service, provide helpful answers, highlight customer best practices, and be a place to find inspirational and strategic insights.

The deployed use cases of your community will determine where you place the greatest emphasis. Educational content to drive product adoption, for example, will likely include many practical tips and tricks on how to use the product. Inspirational content for the same community could include best practice showcases and strategic insights co-created with customers who are advocates in the community. To support your customers in a more human-first way, there may be inspirational stories about how individuals navigated their career paths in a particular industry.

Types of Community Content

Having reviewed the main pillars and purposes of community content, let's dive in a little deeper and consider the content types you can work with when building your community.

Conversations

The bulk of content in an online community is typically made up of conversations. These are generally user-generated discussions that are composed of an initial opening post and a series of replies underneath.

Questions and Answers

The ability to ask a question is central to the power of many kinds of communities. It is the basis of the self-service use case that fuels many digital customer success strategies. On most platforms, the user who asked the question can mark one of the replies as the "best answer," making it easier for other readers with the same question to quickly find the solution. One of the most unique and powerful aspects of communities is that most answers typically come from other customers rather than the company. The rate at which this happens, sometimes termed "the percentage of answers by peers," is an important operational health metric for many communities.

Articles and Blogs

Many communities also contain official long-form articles that share helpful, educational, or inspirational content. These can be authored and published by the company but can also be co-created with customers. The goal of these content types is usually to draw traffic, spark discussion, or provide answers and best practices around popular themes. Communities can also include traditional knowledge base sections for this type of content.

Courses and Trainings

In B2B software, courses and training are increasingly weaved into the community experience to help facilitate onboarding and drive adoption. The main difference with other content types is that courses have a structured learning path with a clear beginning and end. Some might even provide a certificate for the participating user. It's becoming more and more common to see customer education capabilities integrated or connected with the community platform.

Feedback and Ideas

Once you invite customers to be a part of your community, they will undoubtedly give you feedback about your product and the community itself. It's a good idea to welcome any and all feedback and, of course, even better to provide members with a dedicated place in the community for it. Not only does this help to structure the feedback you receive, but it also sends a message to users that you're listening. In your community, you can create sections where customers (or even noncustomers!) can post ideas, and other customers can vote on them. This is a highly scalable and effective way to aggregate product feedback and can solve the fragmentation of feedback channels many product teams struggle with. Complement this with solid cross-functional buy-in to provide the right follow-up and transparency your customers expect.

Product Updates

To drive product adoption, community sections for product and roadmap updates can serve as the central place to learn about new features being released and other roadmap news. In the old pre-SaaS days, this might have been a "release notes" page. Nowadays, this is more likely to be a rich and engaging destination that users can subscribe to and engage with. If your community is set up to invite feedback about your product, it's imperative to also close the feedback loop and communicate what is happening with your product roadmap.

Event-Focused Content

It's also possible to create content through community-focused events. Because most community engagement happens asynchronously, leveraging events will also allow you to add a flavor of synchronous (real-time) engagement. Let's look at two common examples:

- **Ask me anything (AMA):** An AMA session is an engaging format, originally popularized in Reddit communities, where users can ask questions to a subject matter expert in real time. This is a flexible format; the subject matter expert can be anyone from the community manager to someone from the product organization or even your CEO. Questions can be shared up front and moderated to keep the session structured. Plus, the content created in the session can remain in the community as engaging long-tail content that remains popular with readers long after the event.
- **Webinars and office hours:** In recent years, customer success teams and community practitioners have started focusing more time on hosting webinars, which are a great way to add a dynamic and synchronous element to the community. Often this will involve an invited speaker, who could be from your company but could just as well be a customer and member of the community. It's also possible to have the community drive the discussion itself. That's the main premise behind the popular office hours format, where community members are invited to join an open roundtable where they can ask or discuss anything that is top of mind for them.

Social Content

In this chapter, we focus on the content you create on your owned community platform. However, we want to highlight the power and value of amplifying your messages on a social platform such as LinkedIn. As we've seen in previous chapters, we don't recommend building your entire community program on a social media platform, but that doesn't mean those platforms can't play an important role in your overall content strategy.

When leveraging a social platform, we also tap into sheer reach. Our CEO Nick Mehta regularly posts best practices and thought leadership content on LinkedIn, where it garners an extraordinary number of views and a lot of engagement. Tapping into that broader community creates an opportunity to refer back to your owned community platform, inviting interested readers to that central destination where deeper engagement and a more personal experience are possible.

As we've mentioned in previous chapters, the activities that come into play at the very beginning of any kind of community-building involve talking to customers and hosting small live or virtual events. While Nick Mehta can no longer personally talk to or maintain a close personal connection with all of Gainsight's customers, he does have several customer conversations every single week. Those conversations help to determine the focus of his LinkedIn content. This supplement content, combined with deeper engagement and insights in our owned community, maximizes reach.

The same principle can apply to other touchpoints in your customer journey. You might have an active Facebook Group or a Slack community that lives alongside your owned community platform. You can position your community platform as the central destination where the bulk of your company content lives and broadcast relevant topics to the other platforms to amplify your message (reach) and ultimately draw engagement toward your owned platform (depth).

Getting Started with Community Content

Segmenting Your Audience

When creating content for your community, it's helpful to think about customer segments. This will help to ensure that your content strategy is relevant and covers all the needs of the various members of your audience. However, we don't recommend designing a completely new set of personas just for your community. If you already use a set of personas in your company, it's smarter to draw from that existing set. Most B2B SaaS companies will have a very clearly defined set of personas. Your community members will comprise the same prospects and customers you work with at a company level. Making use of the same personas will be helpful in terms of gaining cross-departmental alignment. Suppose you already have an existing set of personas. In that case, it will likely be based on factors like specific customer roles who use your product, potentially combined with company maturity, ARR, product use cases, or customer life cycle stages.

If you are starting from scratch, you can start by looking at data that you have been able to gather around customer demographics, interests, and needs. In a B2B SaaS community, you might consider segments for the various roles within your customers' companies—for example, the admins for your product, those who use your product day to day, or the executive decision-makers in charge of strategy. At Gainsight, we have personas defined for key individuals such as the chief customer officer, the customer success VP, and the Gainsight admin. And we have defined community content, events, and other activities that are relevant for each and every persona. Another way of looking at segmentation could be through the lens of life cycle or maturity of adoption. You could, for instance, create different content segments for onboarding new customers or expert users.

Be wary not to segment too heavily. While it might intuitively seem that a multitude of small segments can help to create more personalized experiences, we find that there are diminishing returns when segments become increasingly small. The level of effort and increased complexity in creating content for many smaller segments can quickly become too much. Instead, focus on a few truly meaningful segments that are clearly differentiated and where different content types will add real value.

Finally, be aware that no segmentation strategy is perfect. It's important to regularly evaluate and fine-tune the approach to ensure that the segmentation strategy is effective and that your content is aligning with your members' needs and interests.

Who Creates Community Content?

How you determine the responsibility for creating content within your community can vary depending on various factors related to your community and your organization. Typically we see that there is a dedicated community manager who is driving the bulk of community initiatives, including those related to content. But there may also be involvement from various departments within the organization.

As we'll see in more detail in Law 6, your community provides exceptional opportunities to break down silos within your organization. Content creation is a prime example of an area where we see marketing, product, and customer success teams coming together to collaborate as part of a content plan, regardless of where the primary ownership of the community lies. The customer success team can often be the best source of great educational content focused on best practices and customer showcases. We increasingly see product teams playing an active role in creating content about features and the roadmap. And the marketing team will often be able to help with content-creation expertise (including visual assets), channels for promotion, as well as with content focused on prospects and expansion.

Deliver Proactive, Personalized, and Relevant Experiences

With the first wave of enterprise communities, content was created with the idea that it would be surfaced reactively when customers searched for it or perhaps when they stumbled across it while browsing. One key development that we want to highlight is the emerging transition in the community space toward more personalization and relevance.

Creating high-quality content that is part of an effective content strategy with clear goals and segments will allow you to utilize email, in-app, social, and other channels to promote content in a highly relevant and personalized way to your customers and their needs. Determining these journeys is at the heart of digital customer success. Essentially, you want to offer the right content to the right customer at the right time. A great example might be a campaign of emails sent over a series of weeks to onboarding customers, offering timely links to content that will help them learn more about your product, adopt its full suite of capabilities, and get maximum value.

Owned community platforms are also increasingly able to surface content within the community in a relevant way based on data that is available about them as part of their member or CRM profile or based on their previous browsing habits. Consider these kinds of capabilities when selecting and setting up your community platform.

We encourage you to move beyond content that lives in silos and consider how every piece of content you create can enrich the broader journey as part of a series of personalized and relevant experiences.

Creating Your Content Plan

Content creation can be complex, particularly if you collaborate internally across multiple teams. So here are some simple, sensible steps that you can take to get started:

1. **Establish content themes:** A good starter exercise is determining a set of content themes with a defined purpose and goal. This ensures that the entirety of your plan is purposeful. You might, for example, start by drawing on the suggestions we have described in this chapter around education and inspiration. Based on those key pillars, you could have a content theme to drive product adoption for a particular segment of

customers. In contrast, another content theme could be aimed at providing advanced best practices for expert users.

2. **Document your plan:** The second step is putting pen to paper in the form of a content plan. This is a strategic document or one-pager that describes all of the content themes with their goals and objectives, along with a calendar for the authoring, publishing, and promotion of the content.

3. **Set up core processes:** If you are a lone wolf community manager, this step might not be needed, but in many cases it is constructive to draft a formal process for creating content. Consider if and how someone will need to review content after it has been authored. Can the authoring be done on a collaboration-friendly platform? Is there going to be a need for an approval step? Who will take care of the publishing itself? Having the process on paper will help things run smoothly when working cross-functionally.

4. **Identify key roles:** Determine who will play a role in the content-creation team. To be truly effective, you will need various skills and expertise, such as writing, editing, visual asset creation, and subject matter expertise from multiple departments. This team will be responsible for the end-to-end content plan—all of which is overseen by the community manager.

5. **Determine metrics of success:** Finally, make sure that your plan includes a method for regularly measuring and analyzing the performance of your content creation efforts. Consider essential metrics such as reach, engagement, and possibly even conversions—all of which depend on the goals that you have set for your content themes. This data can be used to identify areas for improvement and to make adjustments when the results are not what you expected. By being data-driven in this way, you'll be able to swiftly pivot to investing more effort in the types of content that you know work well.

Get Ready to Engage Your Community

In this chapter, we've covered why community content is important and what types of content you can consider creating. We've also walked through some essential steps that you can take to prepare your content plan. Much of this work is fundamental to your community's success, as it will draw members to join, encourage them to participate, and encourage them to return regularly. With the foundation of your content plan in place, you're now ready to look at how to engage meaningfully with your community members and start building real advocacy.

9

Law 5: Build on Your Advocates

Your Most Loyal Customers Are the Gateway to Success

By Remco de Vries and Kenneth Refsgaard

The rise of subscription-based software has made it easy for buyers to sign up for services and explore their capabilities. It has also paved the way for thousands of subscription-based solutions focusing on similar use cases. We have all seen the infographics of the marketing technology landscape showing a map of thousands of tools and services to make the professional lives of marketers easier. Some of them might be technology leaders that are redefining the space with important innovations. Still, most of them are probably similar in capabilities and the problems they aim to solve. So how do you stand out in the middle of an ocean of other tools, and, more importantly, how do you gain a competitive advantage?

Customers are in the market for a product because they have a particular problem they want to solve or an opportunity they want to pursue. It's important to deliver on the expectation that your product will help them do that. But how will they decide if that's the case as they make their purchasing decision? Product-led growth strategies have shown that an easily accessible trial combined with intuitive features can be a powerful and successful approach to growth, but it's not always sufficient. While a trial may demonstrate how the technology works, many SaaS products require some degree of change management and investment before you see actual results. A good example here would be a community platform, where a trial might effectively demonstrate the platform's feature set but can never demonstrate the value of active engagement with customers in the longer term.

So what's the alternative? In the B2B SaaS space, we've observed that prospects want to hear from others who have already implemented the solution and gained value from it. They want to know what they've learned and whether they would recommend their chosen solution. We all know the data points around how much more trustworthy a recommendation from a peer is compared to branded content or a sales pitch. It's no coincidence that G2 has become such an important source of truth in the SaaS world.

What we're talking about is advocacy. It's the incredible power of word-of-mouth recommendations. With a great product and brand, it's possible to generate advocacy organically, based purely on having built something that people love to use and are happy to talk about. But it's also possible to actively develop, nurture, and amplify the depth and reach of this kind of advocacy through skillful engagement with customers. And your community program might just be one of the best places to do that.

Is every happy customer an advocate? The answer to that question, unfortunately, is no. Next to being a happy customer or someone who has succeeded in getting value with your product, being an advocate would mean actively sharing with others. That's an important piece of the puzzle that we can facilitate and nurture. But before we do that, we need to understand what drives advocacy.

What Are Advocates Advocating For?

We believe it's helpful to differentiate between three primary types of advocates. We're looking more deeply at what motivates the behavior of those who are able and willing to advocate for your company and your product.

- **Brand advocates:** Some brands have established a fanbase around them and a mystique that goes far beyond the products themselves. Even if Apple's products aren't always necessarily the most technologically advanced, feature-rich, or offer the greatest value for money, many Apple customers remain loyal out of a deep and long-standing trust in the company and brand. Sometimes there can be a genuine sense of brand advocacy even among those who have never been customers. For example, it's not uncommon to see love and appreciation of Harley-Davidson motorcycles or luxury sports car brands, even from people who have never owned or experienced those products themselves. Brand advocates are likely to think of the companies they love as connected to a particular image, feeling, or lifestyle they want to be associated with.

- **Product advocates:** Product advocates simply love the product and may also love the brand. We've observed that product advocates tend to be experienced customers who enjoy discussing the product with others and sharing their expertise whenever they can. Their interest in and love for the product often mean they are willing to invest significant time in providing feedback and thinking of ways to expand or improve the product. There are many examples on platforms like YouTube, who, for example, offer in-depth guidance and tips about their favorite products and services.

- **Self-advocates:** This one might initially appear out of place, but particularly in the B2B SaaS space, where the use of a product can be deeply intertwined with career development opportunities, we regularly observe those who are engaging in advocacy primarily to build their own personal brand and further their career. While this kind of advocacy is likely less singularly connected to your brand and product, there's a great opportunity in nurturing relationships with these types of customers. Their passion for developing their personal brand likely means they are willing to help co-create content and events with you, which can be a powerful win–win collaboration.

In practice, some of your advocates may fall into more than one of the categories above, of course, and potentially all three. But typically, one of these is the primary motivator of their advocacy activities. This is easily observable in a community platform where you may discover a customer with a tendency to immediately jump into conversations to defend your brand from unfair criticism (a brand advocate), another user with in-depth expertise who often answers questions that other customers have asked (a product advocate), and another customer who contributes novel thought leadership and success stories (a self-advocate). These activities are incredibly valuable and likely to happen in some shape or form for all companies delivering a quality product or service. However, if you actively nurture advocacy, you will tap into the opportunity to amplify the impact and value of what these incredible customers are doing.

Nurturing Advocacy Activities

You can actively encourage and nurture several advocacy activities as part of your community program. Let's consider four of the most important ones:

- **Peer-to-peer support.** In the first wave of enterprise communities, advocacy generally always meant one simple thing— the willingness of a group of community experts to answer questions in their free time. As we've seen above, these are typically product advocates with deep expertise and product experience. They can be profoundly passionate and critical, sometimes leading to a situation where they are actively helping other customers while acting in some ways as a brand detractor toward your company. When that happens, we like to reflect that their frustration is rooted in a deep care for your product and investment in the direction it is evolving. Product advocates tend to get satisfaction from recognition of their expertise, which is why the traditional approach to nurturing this type of activity has been around gamification mechanisms and elevated status within the community platform. These tried and tested approaches remain highly effective today.

- **Innovation and product feedback.** Another area product advocates will tend to gravitate toward is in delivering thoughtful product feedback and ideas. Product advocates' innate motivation and interest means that this kind of feedback will be shared through any and all available channels, whether invited or not—for example, through support tickets or to your CSM. A community platform, however, offers many ways to engage with and promote this kind of activity in a scalable way. By opening up the possibility of sharing ideas and votes in the community, you will quickly spot your product advocates as the ones generating the majority of feedback. These advocates will respond well to further engagement and invitations to, for example, your beta testing programs or small innovation-focused events. By maintaining this kind of engagement, they are also likely to help manage and consolidate feedback that's coming in from other customers. A wonderful dynamic we often observe is that once product advocates have been invited to a beta testing or other innovation program, they tend to be more positive about new releases, advocate publicly, and provide peer-to-peer guidance when those new product capabilities are rolled out.

- **Webinars and live events.** As we've touched on above, some of your customers will be looking to develop their careers and personal brand. If they are at least to some degree also product or brand advocates, you have an opportunity to engage them and invite them to webinars or live events where they can speak publicly. This is a practice that we see many B2B SaaS companies adopt, because it takes us to the heart of the principle that content from a peer is more trustworthy than branded content. Stories from customers can be presented in this way to serve numerous use cases and goals, such as presenting the value of your product to an audience of prospects or sharing success stories aimed at increasing adoption among existing customers. One of the powerful aspects of this type of engagement is that you are truly giving back to your advocates, because they will get tangible value by demonstrating their knowledge and speaking skills publicly, potentially leading directly to new career opportunities, while you, of course, are benefiting from the generation of trustworthy and engaging content—a true win-win!

- **References, case studies, and referrals.** As part of the sales process for just about every SaaS product, there will be constant requests for customer references and case studies. Every prospect will want to hear from someone who isn't directly trying to sell to them to get the unvarnished truth before making their decision. The community itself can be a great place for prospects to gather this intelligence. Still, you can also leverage the community to identify existing customers willing to act as references and co-create content with you. This is where you'll be on the lookout for those brand advocates who also have a degree of product knowledge and expertise. It's important to note that your advocates also have their own networks and are likely to provide positive referrals and directly promote your product to people they know without any prompting on your part. This effect will be amplified by the case studies and events you involve your advocates in, as their opinions will be sought out directly.

Developing an Advocacy Strategy and Program

We've already touched on many essential themes around who your advocates are, what motivates them, and the kinds of activities they will likely engage in. The next thing to consider is how to nurture and maximize the impact of their activities. We recommend designing and implementing a structured strategy and program to do this.

The first thing to consider is how you will identify advocates in an organized way. You may already know several advocates through their engagement with your posts on social media platforms such as LinkedIn or simply through the relationships established with them as customers. Advocates may show up in many ways, and these are just a couple of examples. A key element in your advocacy program, however, will be to proactively identify upcoming and potential advocates in which your community platform will be influential.

One of the great things about enterprise community platforms is that their native gamification systems are fine-tuned to motivate and inspire ongoing engagement through providing rewards and recognition and data and insight into customers who are starting to demonstrate advocacy behaviors. This might mean, for example, rising through the levels of a ranking structure or being the winner of a points leaderboard system. Monitoring these systems will provide early signals that there's an opportunity to engage and nurture.

Beyond gamification, it can be helpful to monitor community data to help determine which customers are on the path to becoming advocates. We often recommend thinking of community engagement as a funnel. Danny Pancratz, community director at Unqork, has designed one of our favorite examples of an "engagement funnel." It illustrates the path from a visiting customer all the way to someone who is formally advocating on behalf of Unqork by speaking at events or through testimonials. Every stage in this model is quantifiable and based on tangible data.

Engagement Funnel   Aware→Adopts→Active→Advocates

All Visitors (Registered + Guests)	**Visits the Community** Logged-in or out; Known or Unknown
Registered Visitors (+ New Registrations)	**Visits the Community: Is Known** Tracking cookie from previous log-in
Active Users	**1+ Active Visits** Logs-in for full access to forums, etc.
Recurring Users	**Active on 3+ Unique Days** Demonstrates repeated activitvy
Contributing Users	**Contributes Activity** Posts, Replies, Upvotes, etc.
SMEs	**Highly Active over 3+ Months** Also achieves 20+ accepted answers
Speakers & Testimonials	**Advocates on Our behalf** Event speakers, testimonial blogs, etc.

Having put in place mechanisms to identify potential advocates, we recommend designing a structured program for engaging with them. A central theme at the heart of a program like this is recognition. In the first wave of enterprise communities, the foundation of a superuser program was the creation of a private area in the community and a public title in the community, such as "VIP," "Champion," or "Rock Star." The private area would be used for deeper engagement with the advocates, where they might be given early access to information about upcoming product news and direct access to the team behind the community. Members of a program like this would often receive birthday or Christmas cards and might get invited to company events or other in-person gatherings.

Programs like this have tended to be geared toward maximizing peer-to-peer support activity, and they are often highly effective at doing that. They're particularly effective when the program is recognized at all levels of the company. Erica Kuhl shared a superb example with us from the early days of the Salesforce Trailblazer community. She told us, "We started our first superuser program, and I remember running into our CEO, who said, 'Hey, what are you doing with those MVPs (Most Valuable Professionals) when you're not at Dreamforce?' And I said, 'Well, we don't really come back together except for Dreamforce.' When I returned to my desk, he sent me his cost center number. So we flew them all to San Francisco for our first MVP summit. Our CEO lined up every single one of his executives to parade through that event and present their roadmaps. All the superusers were under NDA, and we wanted their feedback." Needless to say, the Salesforce MVP program is still going strong today.

As the community space has evolved, we have seen an ongoing evolution in B2B SaaS communities where customers have a deeper connection to brands and products due to them being so closely connected to their career path. The Salesforce Trailblazer community is a phenomenal example of this. Another great example, as we can see in Danny Pancratz's engagement funnel above, is the subject matter expert (SME) program at the heart of the Unqork community. This is a formal program where community members can become SMEs through ongoing participation and helping other community members by answering their questions. In a B2B SaaS community, becoming an SME or MVP can be meaningful and valuable in a way that extends far beyond the community itself. Pancratz often celebrates new SMEs outside of the community by posting on LinkedIn, and those customers are likely to mention their membership in the program on their CVs and in job applications. He has evidence that the Unqork SME program has helped community members to gain promotions and new jobs.

As a fun sidenote, Pancratz himself is one of the most active contributors in our own community and is someone we consider an advocate. In addition to our close partnership with him as a customer, we invited him to be a speaker at our annual Pulse conference, where he also has won one of our Gamechangers awards. This is advocacy in action.

The Impact and Value of Advocacy

We've already looked at the idea of an engagement funnel, a powerful data-driven way to measure how deeply customers engage in a community. What this model doesn't tell us, however, is the impact of those advocacy activities. The best way to look at value and impact will depend on the type of advocacy activity that is nurtured:

- **Peer-to-peer support.** This activity, driven by your product advocates, will help you scale and find efficiencies by increasing support ticket deflection and maximizing the reach of your helpful self-service content. A great indicator that your program is starting to deliver value in this direction is the percentage of answers in the community that the members of your advocacy program are creating. This can be as high as 80% or above in some communities.
- **Product feedback and innovation.** The activities of your advocates related to product feedback will help to accelerate your rate of innovation. Your product team will discover tremendous efficiencies in aggregating feedback because they will need to spend less time on fragmented feedback sources. Just as significantly, this activity will help to drive increased product adoption.
- **References, case studies, and referrals.** For these types of activities driven by your brand advocates, there will be an amplification of the efforts of your marketing and sales teams. You'll see this in the volume of referrals and case studies being generated and in improvements to the results and scalability of marketing and sales efforts.
- **Events and webinars.** Many of your events and webinars will be aimed at prospects, and you will directly see an impact in your pipeline. However, these activities can also profoundly amplify self-service and drive increased product adoption.

These are just a few examples of the value and impact you can expect once you start nurturing advocacy activities in an organized way. In Law 9, we will look at the business value of your community program in much more depth and detail.

Platform, Content, Advocacy: What's Next?

In the last few chapters, we have covered many of the essential building blocks of an effective community program. It's now time to explore the broader and deeper question of who in your company owns and runs all of these important elements. Is your community program simply owned and run by a person or a team? In our next chapter, we will find out.

10

Law 6: Everybody Owns the Customer

Community Is a Company-Wide Strategy, Not a Department

By Seth Wylie

Community is a strange initiative. One small team is *responsible* for it, but the entire company *owns* it *together*. It's impossible to picture the makeup of a team who can represent all the interests of your customers, prospects, and partners. So how do you construct these partnerships between the community team and so many others? And which department should hold the community team so that it can make the biggest impact?

Community Starts at the Top, with a Purpose

Gainsight became an example of a company-wide commitment to the community when we hosted our first Pulse conference in 2013. Each year, our CEO, Nick Mehta, reminisces from the keynote stage about that small gathering and about how Pulse has grown. He radiates pride, enthusiasm, and earnest goodwill for the customer success community. His calendar backs that up with uncountable customer calls, networking and career coaching conversations, community events, and more. His support even came full circle, fueling our first-ever deep integration between the in-person Pulse experience and Gainsight's virtual community platform.

Dean Stoecker, now executive chairman, was CEO of the analytics automation company Alteryx in 2015. He said, "No one's ever going to learn our product if we don't allow customers some frictionless environment to share and communicate with each other. . . . Customers don't want to call up tech support and ask questions. They want to talk to experts who are in their field. Maybe they're in the same geography. Maybe they're in the exact same vertical with the same use case. They want to talk to those people" (Magwaza, 2022).

At the same time, Alteryx's chief customer officer, Matthew Stauble, sees that buy-in when the board asks for a community update at every meeting. He also sees that from his fellow executives and in his day-to-day work. "Every single customer that I talk to, community comes up." The community is packed with inspiring use cases and tactical advice, but something extra shows up with the Alteryx Certified Experts (ACEs), who are "passionate about the product and [how] it changes lives." When asked about how executives across so many departments get excited about community, Stauble says that they see the incredible impact of their tool on the world. One customer used Alteryx analysis automation to literally save lives, by accurately administering cancer medication. Others predict market fluctuations that save their companies sums with an astonishing number of zeroes. Stauble describes that the executive team and customers see that there is life-changing power when you get the heavy lifting of analysis out of the way, allowing the *insights* of the analytics to shine through.

Your community comprises people who share the same purpose that your executives champion. The belief that you're doing something important, something of value, can link together all the characters in your wildly diverse community, including your employees across all teams. If you don't have an executive champion for community yet, then your work starts with sharing those stories of purpose with executives who personally care about the impact your business is having on the world. Show them the people with whom they share that. Every year at Pulse, Gainsight hears one top takeaway from first-timers and even repeat attendees. They're taken aback, a bit astonished. "I'm not alone," they say.

Community's Value Flows in All Directions

Employees have nearly as much freedom to dodge engaging in community as customers and prospects do. Another priority will always win—even just their inbox—unless the community feels personally beneficial to them. Thankfully, employees can reap the same enticing benefits as customers and prospects, though they manifest differently. A community is a pathway for employees and members to exchange rewarding interactions in a perpetual loop.

The first "loop" that drives employee engagement includes valuable information, expertise, and empowerment. Employees contribute their subject matter knowledge, coaching, and a listening ear to customers and prospects. Meanwhile, customers return the favor, describing real-world use cases, sharing feedback, and serving as case studies and references. Employees and customers alike are offering networking that provides knowledge and inspiration. This "value loop" benefits everyone by helping them with their job, responsibilities, goals, and extrinsic motivations. Operating alone, this loop can keep everyone coming back.

The second community positive feedback loop is made of enthusiasm, validation, and inclusion. Employees create community spaces where community members feel that they can express exactly how jazzed they are about the configuration conundrum they just solved, their idea for a new initiative, or anything that only these people in this community could possibly celebrate, let alone understand. Moreover, employees congratulate and reward them, and amplify their voice through platforms like webinars, case studies, and more. They also show that within this big company with all its authority in the market, someone knows them, cares about what they're doing, and values their contribution.

Meanwhile, customers provide employees with plenty of validation, too. Employees spend their days solving problems for customers, building tools for them, negotiating agreeable contract terms, and so much more. When those customers do amazing things and show how much it helped their success in their job, in their career, or even, in Alteryx's case, saving lives, then every bit of work feels worth far more than the paycheck. This "validation loop" benefits everyone by showing them that their work matters to real humans, leaving them with an intense gut-level sense of drive. Unrestricted by department, responsibilities, or relationship to your company, everyone in the community becomes anchored to your company's purpose, championed by your executives.

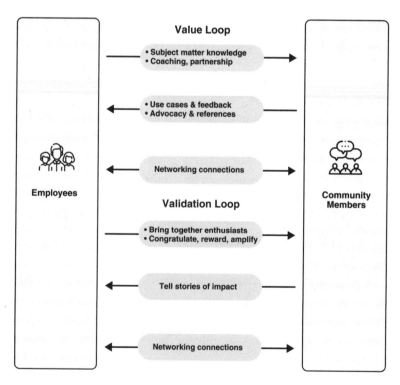

Engage Employees in the Value Loop

When Gainsight hosts its Pulse conference, employees' weeks are packed. There are happy hours with customers, lunch roundtables, box seats with VIPs from customers and prospects, networking between sessions, and more. In-person attendees also dive into Pulse's virtual spaces, including our online community. No employee would dream of saying, "Maybe my time would be better spent answering emails." At in-person events, the validation loop sweeps everyone away. For a community to hold its own in the everyday prioritization death-match, though, each department needs to see a line of impact running from the community to its business goals. And as we have seen in Chapter 4, every department can benefit from a community, whether it's customer success, support, marketing, or product teams.

You must adapt the value loop to each level of the organization to build buy-in. Reporting to the C-suite should focus on lagging outcomes that have dollar signs. If your community is focused on success, for example, then they'll want to see the net retention rate of customers engaged in the community versus those who are not. The VP- and director-level will focus more on leading indicators that they feel more agency to impact (like Net Promoter Score®), and activities that contribute to them (like number of engaged members). Individual contributors will want to know exactly how community is influencing their responsibilities. For example, provide a CSM with a report of their customers who are most and least engaged on community.

With a clear understanding of the impact that community should have on their goals, employees can be thoughtful about how to engage. They can also more clearly identify community activity that helps them, understand the impact they are having personally, and tell leadership how they're making the most of the community that the company has invested in creating.

Engage Employees in the Validation Loop

The community team at collaboration software company Miro, at first glance, lives in a fantasy utopia of effortless community centricity.

According to Shira Galler Re'em, head of community success (speaking from the back of her unicorn), "Everyone thinks of that end user and our community who advocates for us, who champions for us, who speaks on our behalf. They know how important, how real that build-up is, so they really keep it in mind in everything they're doing." Miro's community story, though, begins in 2020. Marina Perminova, now community operations and strategy manager, was on Miro's support team. When Miro had just 100 employees, she saw customers' stories travel easily among employees, including to the CEO. "We never had to prove the value that we should have community, or that we should build the community team. Our leadership initiated this conversation."

This sense of urgency to nurture community is the output of the validation loop. A support ticket or NPS survey response would stun them, showing what Miro meant to customers' purposes in their roles and careers. Galler Re'em says, "Any time a CEO would step in, it was always personal. . . . It was always like the CEO really cared on a personal level for the people that told them their stories." One moment of feeling that validation leads to sending some swag in the mail and, importantly, feeling great about it. Nowadays, leadership throughout Miro notices success stories on social media, and company-wide meetings regularly feature community members as guest speakers. Generate buy-in and partnership for community by regularly jolting employees with stories that show impact on humans, not ROI. As these moments accumulate, you'll find more and more of the company eager to get involved in the community, and even feeling like they belong.

Start Small, with Eager Believers

Nisha Baxi, head of community at Gong, joined the organization and launched their community within 90 days. During that time, Baxi did a "road show," meeting individually with every department head, and every member of the executive leadership team. Largely, those conversations involved teaching: what the community was going to be, how it would impact their area of the business, and how their department could help. Then Baxi ventured further. "I trained up everyone. 'This is the art of the possible. Will you just try this with me? Will you experiment? Let's just try it for a week and see how it goes. Let's try it for a month and see how it goes.' Because no one knows. As a community professional, you do. So you show people, you train them, and then over time, people will come up with ideas." Baxi brought the first ideas to the table. The only thing she needed from the other teams was interest.

As Baxi made her initial rounds, she was looking out for her potential advocates. They reveal themselves through their questions, comments, and even just earnest eye contact. They are the people to approach with an idea for a quick win. A first, small project makes the most of the initial flush of enthusiasm, and also gauges if they'll give the bit of effort that this low-hanging fruit needs from them.

Baxi saw an opportunity in Gong's support team, for example. They were burdened with capturing feature requests. Baxi did the heavy lifting. She created the Google Form for customers to submit requests and asked where it should fit in the support workflow. She asked what customers should be told when directed to the form, and then she wrote the copy. Support provided guidance and trained their team. The Google Form was later replaced by an ideation category in their online community, and Gong's customer feature requests now feed directly into the product team's backlog for prioritization. "How I was able to get adoption internally was to not just explain the art of the possible, but to show them, and show that you really believe that this will be impactful." She sums up the reaction of the chief product officer and co-founder's reaction to the customer input: "This is insane. I've never seen anything like this. This is awesome." He supported the backlog integration, and checks the requests himself proactively. Baxi has since used the same technique to build bridges with teams across the company.

Crank up the Momentum

With some quick wins and a few newborn advocates, the next challenge is to do *more*. If a team's commitment to community is only as big as the most recent project, though, then you're always battling other priorities and shiny new ideas. Or, if you rely on a strong advocate, then you're left to start all over when they leave the organization. You get past these risks by making everything about other teams' goals. As Nisha Baxi says, you "follow the music."

Jillian Bejtlich, community lead at Calendly and former director of community at Zapier, describes how, when she started, community was sitting in a silo and being disconnected from the rest of the company. Now she works hard to make sure her community team is in the know about the goals of the departments they serve, so they can identify areas where they can make a difference. The average stakeholder has little understanding of how a community works and is unpracticed at imagining how they can be used. It's the community team's responsibility to provide that imagination and expertise. Bejtlich is succinct, "It's never about us. We are enablers."

To help the business find those opportunities, Bejtlich sets up her teammates to be the bridges to other departments. One person works on product update posts, positioning them up to build rapport with product. Another works on community moderation, which is the perfect spot to nurture a relationship with support. By building so many connections to other parts of the organization—instead of all of those threads flowing through her—Bejtlich sees conversations that reveal business goals happening "constantly."

Having found an opportunity to support a business goal, the next step is to craft the community-led program that suits the need. In the case of the "quick wins," the best solutions are time-tested, simple community engagement techniques. In contrast, when a department describes a large, complex goal, it merits a bespoke community program. The solution-crafting process needs to be conversational and consultative. The community team should provide proactive suggestions to get the ball rolling, but they also must listen and invent.

Bejtlich's team collaborated with marketing to generate conversation based on new messaging. Marketing then witnessed the quality of the conversations and search traffic to them. They later approached the community team proactively to be part of more campaigns. The ability to build trust through collaborative projects is critical to community management.

Cross-functional partners are also in the dark about the goings-on in your community that they would care about deeply. Once a community team understands the goals and priorities of other departments, they are empowered to use their deep visibility into the community to identify knowledge that deserves to be shared.

- At the most tactical level, the community team should share critical information. Product would want to hear without delay that their brand-new feature is painfully slow on mobile devices. Customer success would want to know that a large customer is struggling.
- The team should also be looking for valuable anecdotes. Does marketing want to turn this highly viewed post into a case study or invite the author to speak on a webinar? Might services want to add this creative and easy use case to onboardings?
- Nearly any department would value themes and trends. This could be a gradual increase in activity around a certain feature, increased sign-ups by a key persona, or woe-is-me comments about a feature that's being sunsetted.

The community team's filtering and processing of the community's always-on, ever-shifting activity is essential in creating cross-functional buy-in. They might even configure their community analytics tools to extract that information more easily or provide up-to-the-minute reporting. Stakeholders will feel that they don't merely have the community available for their initiatives but that they receive unexpected nuggets of golden insights. Moreover, they must feel that the community isn't an agent of chaos and hidden risks. Instead, if something important were to come up, they would hear about it.

Strengthen cross-functional buy-in with metrics. "There is an increased activity about Feature X" has less impact than "35% increase in posts." Stakeholders will want to see their value loop metrics, plus the quantity and quality of activity in programs they care about. Leadership will want to know that the community is healthy and growing. Metrics help all departments and all levels of the organization see, interpret, and believe in the activities that are going on.

As one final tactic to ensure the rubber meets the road on cross-functional buy-in, Bejtlich casually makes the circuit of Zapier's leadership each quarter. She builds relationships, learns about their goals, and hears about their major initiatives. She may offer some suggestions about how the community team could help, and they might collaborate in the moment on ideas for programs. She also shares news from the community, whether about developments in the platform and programs or about trends and metrics. As a result of these conversations, she has even been invited to recurring leadership meetings in some departments, so community always has a seat at the table. Her team may build cross-functional bridges at a tactical level, but she supplements it at the management level, and even makes sure to keep the C-suite on board. "They've got so much on their plates, but I have done my rounds. They know that we exist. They're huge advocates for community."

Community Management Skills

Let's say that you've had unmitigated success at engaging every single department in the validation and value loops. You've found your advocates and earned quick wins. You're integrating community into their plans to achieve their business goals every quarter. You're on fire! Except you still need a team to make it all happen! Let's break down the skill sets and organizational structure you need to create a vibrant community, and to orient it toward the business goals of each department.

Program Leadership

To launch programs that support other teams' goals, your community team needs skills in cross-functional relationship-building and leading through influence. They will also need enough understanding of community management to serve up specific ideas for programs. Creativity and experimentalism will allow them to craft bespoke programs. Lastly, they need the skills to measure and communicate the program's success.

Community Leadership

An inventive program is useless without a vibrant community to engage in, so the community team must also nurture the community in general. They will design the new member onboarding experience, for example. They also would need to identify that the onboarding experience would be the most important thing to focus on at the moment. So they need to understand how healthy communities work, how to measure community health, and how to create strategic programs to improve it.

Tummeling

When a person tells you, "That's so interesting. Do you know who you should talk to? So-and-so was working on that exact thing last month," you feel a special cocktail of gratitude, discovery, and promise. That person is "tummeling." When running community programs, your "tummelers" are constantly scanning for opportunities to @-mention just the right people, post interesting information or discussion questions, or offer some benevolent rabble-rousing. ("You should write a post about that! People would love it." "Everyone is asking about this topic; we should host a webinar." "Let me dig into recent posts and see who seems to be an expert in that feature.") They generate conversation in a way that feels enthusiastic, genuine, and organic, instead of artificial and like an advertisement. Tummeling also includes moderation: elegant interventions when activity is counterproductive or violates community guidelines.

Community Operations

When your community team envisions a way that they want to interact with the community or with teams internally, they need to invent the tools to make it happen. They need to be conversant in software, data, success metrics, the workflows of the community team and other departments, your documentation, and community best practices.

The Team Can Be One or Many

Nisha Baxi from Gong is the quintessential first community hire. She brought skills across program leadership, community leadership, tummeling, and community operations. She assessed the bigger picture, but also did the detailed heavy lifting, including non-scalable, one-on-one interactions with internal stakeholders, community members, and potential members.

You get to choose skills to emphasize in your first hire. Customers of cybersecurity companies, for example, can be wary of interacting; the community will need impressive tummeling. Or, if the focus of the community is to improve product quality, you can just put your community team within product and lower your standards on cross-functional program leadership skills.

Your next hire, or even several hires, will be community managers focused on tummeling. They may be generalists across your programs, or specialize in moderation, content creation, gamification, superusers and advocates, or certain sectors of the community. Your needs will reveal themselves from the work of your first hire.

It's easy to wait too long before creating a community operations role. Watch for pinch points where teammates are spending too much time just getting the work done, or never finding time for fundamentals like reporting or upgrading the community platform. A community operations expert releases the team from the drag of weak processes and tools. Along with their expertise in software, data, and so on, you get to look for extraordinary systems thinking, consultative problem-solving, process design, and enablement. They will assume basic responsibilities like managing your community platform and reporting. They will also find and fix areas of inefficiency so everyone on the team becomes more efficient and effective. They will help you measure impact and thus substantiate your community budget.

The development of a community team's responsibilities will parallel the development of the community itself. For detailed recommendations on how to nurture a community at different levels of maturity, the team can lean on books like *Buzzing Communities* by Richard Millington (2012).

So, Who Owns Community?

It's time to face reality: while engagement and passion for your community can be distributed across your company, your community team still needs to live somewhere. There is no one answer to this question. The most relevant department will be best suited to shape the community's strategy, to measure its impact, and to build relationships with mission-critical stakeholders.

Standalone Community Org, Owned at the C-Level

A few organizations have launched the innovation of a chief community officer, and others have a less senior community leader reporting to the CEO. These companies are unwilling to tilt the balance toward product, or marketing, or customer success, or support. Although a new community can never build all things at once, an independent department is best positioned to create a holistic strategy to redirect the impact of community wherever the business most needs it and eventually build strength in all areas. This structure requires the CEO's active support to build buy-in since no department will have the motivation that comes from being the sole autonomous beneficiary.

Community in Product

You will collect troves of product feedback, ranging from "Is this a bug?" to "I need to do XYZ, but it's impossible" to pie-in-the-sky concepts. Reactions to product changes will be immediate. Customers will feel that their needs impact the product roadmap. Product managers will prioritize and design improvements that better suit customers' needs.

Although it could make sense to have community owned by product teams in the startup life, in our experience, though, nearly every community has broader goals, and is therefore owned by teams *other* than product, even if product is highly engaged.

Community in Marketing

In our experience, in about a quarter of companies, the community is owned by marketing. Inspiration will be the name of the game every day. Expect professional-grade content about the exact business challenges most burdening your target market(s). Discussions of use cases will be broad, since the community will draw noncustomers into conversations facilitated by community managers who are not experts in implementing your product. It will be hard, or even alienating, to get deep into product functionality. You will have greater respect in the market and create a rich well of advocates and case studies. The community will generate and nurture leads, and grease the wheels in sales cycles.

Community in the Customer Team

Three-quarters of communities that we've seen are owned in the customer organization.

If it sits in customer success, your community will be most concerned with questions of what customers could or should do. This may be related to a functionality ("What's the first way that you used this feature?"), to overall use cases ("How do you use the product to help with such-and-such business goal?") to success unrelated to the product ("What are you focusing on nowadays?" or "Does anyone know a candidate for our open role?") and even to career advice ("What online courses would you recommend?"). This takes workload off your CSMs, and even provides inspiration and credible advice beyond what customers normally receive from you.

Or, if community lives in support, discussions will be focused on reactive answers to tactical product questions. This includes explanations of features, troubleshooting, and suggestions for how to use the product for a certain goal. It takes workload off your support team, and customers even get answers to questions that they wouldn't have bothered to submit in a ticket. Of all the options, this one includes the least "inspiration" in the mix.

In other words, community responsibilities are distributed across teams, with a central community function. This is what Erica Kuhl experienced. "Now, there are community representatives in many different organizations within Salesforce. They did not report to me, they reported to their businesses, but my KPIs all aligned to theirs. Their success and governance were all managed by me at a central place, but they were getting all the value from the community for their department. No one asks anymore, is community my job? It is their job. It's just not even a question."

To summarize, here is some final wisdom from Talia Goldberg, partner at Bessemer Venture Partners: "If your community is mostly targeted towards your customers, it should sit in the customer organization. And whether that's within customer success, support, or broadly as sitting under a CRO, that is typically where the community should sit. If your community is extremely broad and much larger than your customer base, it probably sits either as a standalone function or in the marketing team."

Who's Excited?

Community management is a new type of motion for your business. At moments it will feel strange, experimental, and vague. Which leader gets most excited about the impact that community can have? That belief will carry them through the natural uncertainty of doing something new, especially since community's impact takes time to become visible. That leader will also be less likely to drop the community slide from the all-hands deck, more likely to suggest that a person flag an opportunity for the community team, and lean toward community with all those other tiny decisions that accumulate to real impact. Lastly, for a community team to turn their potential into success, they need time and creativity. They will be hard-pressed to find either if they feel the threat that their own management needs convincing that community even has potential. Do your community a favor and make sure that the department's leadership believes in it.

Connecting Your Whole Company to Community

Even when a community is owned by a single team, it should still be a cross-functional effort and aligned strategy. According to Patrick Smith, chief marketing officer at Cvent: "One of the things I pushed for was this cannot just be a marketing thing. I need commitments with SLAs from other parts of the organization, from product and customer success specifically, that they're going to want to contribute and are going to proactively manage the community with us. Because while it's driven by marketing, it goes far beyond us."

Any new community also runs the risk of being relegated to an isolated corner, pleading for attention and engagement from their colleagues, as they watch the glimmers of enthusiasm from customers and prospects float by, just out of reach. You avoid this outcome by turning the community into a central clearinghouse of motivating, valuable conversation for employees, even as it benefits external members. The *ownership* of community, then, is company-wide. The *responsibility* for the community spaces rests on your community team, who you've hired for the skills as cross-functional coordinators, connectors, and leaders, regardless of which team they report to. When done well, you'll find leaders across the organization delighted with the benefits of community, and full of ideas for how it can help them reach their goals.

So far, we mainly talked about building your community online. But there is more in the world than our digital screens. In the next chapter, we will expand our mindset and talk about how offline community building can strengthen your broader community program.

11

Law 7: Offline Counts More Than You Think

An Online Community Is Strengthened with Offline Events

By Erin Rhodes and Robin Merritt

We started this book by discussing the galvanizing communities many of us experience as consumers—working at a local coffee shop, watching your favorite sports team in an arena, or seeing Taylor Swift in concert (or other non-Taylor artist faves). There is something special about all of these communities: the magic of in-person human connection.

While we have shared our learnings on the incredible power of online communities—in terms of scale, personalization, access, inclusion, and more—we have learned that nothing beats the power of mixing online *and* offline communities.

Why do you need to worry about offline communities? Aren't "events" such a dated concept? In our experience, in-person events are more important and impactful than ever for several reasons:

- **Connection:** While "follows," "friends," and "likes" online can generate a temporary shot of dopamine in your brain, technology still hasn't figured out how to replicate the warmth of an in-person smile, the feeling of a handshake, or the comfort of a hug. In Law 10, we'll talk about building culture and values into your community. This is so much more powerful if your community has laughed and learned together in real life. Get your customers together in person, and they will leave more connected.
- **Focus:** The technology world is ever more—*sorry, hold on, I have to check Twitter*—distracted. We all see this in video conference meetings with our teammates and clients. Everyone has their own trick to pretend they are paying attention, but most are furiously typing away and spending about 10% of their active brain capacity on the meeting at hand. As such, virtual events, online communities, and digital happy hours struggle for one thing: attention. By comparison, having your clients locked in a room (well, maybe not literally) thinking about one topic has a profound effect on their future behavior.
- **FOMO:** One of the best parts of offline events is simply that each attendee sees all of the other people and thinks, "If these folks are here, I should be paying attention." The not-so-scientific term for this is FOMO (fear of missing out). In general, businesses launch communities to drive customer behavior—whether that's buying new products, adopting services, or getting more value from the vendor. If your customers are in a packed room together, they'll leave feeling like they should be doing more.

The key point we want to make is that the question isn't online *or* offline—it's that online *and* offline is a magical combination.

At Gainsight, we built our company early on largely through in-person events of various kinds. In that process, we've studied the offline community strategies of other industry leaders like Salesforce.com, Marketo, Gong, and many more companies. We'll share a taxonomy of strategies for offline communities and then a plethora of "pro tips" for each strategy.

But before we do that, we'll start with the big idea.

The Big Idea: Change Your "Why" for Events

Events are not a new concept in B2B businesses. Most of us have had the misfortune of having walked trade show floors, getting accosted by booth staff, collecting and then quickly throwing away plastic tchotchkes, and receiving hundreds of spam emails right after we leave. And then there are the monotonic panels where everyone agrees with one another, presenters read off slides in six-point font full of animation and clip art but signifying nothing, and agendas packed so tightly that you can't do the one thing you actually are there for—meeting other people. Have you been there, or is it just me?

Why do most B2B events (pardon my French) suck? The answer is simple: they have the wrong "why."

Most B2B companies look at events as a "marketing" tactic. Marketers are looking for "leads." So they create a veneer of a conference with the main goal of getting your email address. They only invite prospective clients, because "Why would we waste money on customers?" They create the content as a thinly veiled sales pitch. Then find a soulless and cheap venue and use the same "paint-by-numbers" playbook as every other company. And they get what they should expect—fake metrics about leads (mostly from people who didn't realize they even gave out their email), a high-five on a "successful show," and a plan to do it the same way next year.

There is another way. Community-first business leaders (maybe like you) play the long game. They realize you have to give to get.

Events aren't a tactical and transactional way to get email addresses. They are a vehicle to give your clients value by offering them the connections, learning, and inspiration they desire most. Events are about becoming strategic to your clients.

And guess what? If your clients view you as strategic, they will:

- Buy more quickly from you
- Buy more from you
- Stay longer with you
- Become bigger advocates

To make this chapter actionable, let's go through some of our learnings around events—from small to big—and include our best "pro tips."

Start Small: Lunches and Dinners

When you hear "events," you might think, "I'm not ready for that." In your mind, perhaps you imagine Salesforce's Dreamforce conference, with tens of thousands of attendees. Or maybe for you the image is the Super Bowl.

If we were advising someone on starting an offline component to building a community, we would say: start with meals.

Over the years, we have bought a lot of food at Gainsight. We have hosted hundreds and hundreds of meals—breakfasts, lunches, and dinners—to bring our target audience (customer success leaders) together.

The goal is always similar: gather like-minded individuals to connect and learn. That's it. But if you interview our clients who ended up purchasing our software, many consider events like these as part of the value of working with us. They want to be part of our "community."

Nick is notoriously maniacal about these sessions, because he thinks, rightfully so, that details are everything to create the right vibe. As such, here is our secret list of "pro tips":

Venue

- Pick a private room, if possible, so that you can have one conversation.
- Ask the staff to turn the music down or off.
- Choose a room with the right "geometry." If it's a small dinner, a 6- to 8-person round table is amazing. If it's bigger, 10 to 20 at a longer table is fine, but don't make it too big or you can't have a dialogue.

Invites

- Build your invite list thoughtfully. Try to pick people from similar companies or roles so there is a high-quality conversation. We use LinkedIn to filter on city and title.
- Test over time and figure out how many people you have to invite to get to the right attendee count. For us, if we want to host 10 people, we might invite 50, expect 15 to confirm, and 10 to show up.
- Consider the invite coming directly from the executive in your company who is hosting, versus coming from marketing or sales. For example, for Nick's events, the emails come from Nick.
- We have attendees RSVP simply by replying to Nick and his executive assistant. Web form signups make events less intimate.
- In the invite, include basic logistical details and a rough agenda.
- Consider a second email to people who didn't reply to the first one, including a list of people who have RSVPed thus far. FOMO FTW!

Agenda

- After seating, we try to have one discussion as a group.
- We always start with an icebreaker question (e.g., "What was your childhood dream?").
- We then typically have a few topics based on the theme of the event.

- We often close with "one-word checkout"—one word to describe how you feel leaving this event. The only rule is that you can't repeat others' words!

Hosting
- This is the biggest part—whoever is hosting needs to actually act as a host.
- That person should be there early, greet guests, and connect people together prior to seating.
- The host should carefully think through seating, potentially aligning key prospective clients next to relevant happy, existing customers.
- We recommend asking everyone to have one conversation during dinner, starting with intros and icebreakers, moving to content, and then the closing checkout.
- We aspire to give everyone a voice and try to direct opportunities to let everyone speak.

Post-Event
- We always send a follow-up thank-you note, including some relevant recent blog posts.
- We also try to capture notes and create a social post with learnings with a photo from the event. This amplifies the effect of the event and brings more people to future events.
- Finally, as a bonus, we sometimes note answers to the icebreaker and send gifts tied to the theme. For example, to this day one customer remembers getting a US Postal Service Halloween costume in the mail after he stated his childhood dream was to be a mailman!

Crowdsource: Meetups

In parallel, as you build your community, consider having your community amplify your event strategy. In the consumer world, this is the entire premise of MeetUp.com and similar websites.

In the B2B world, you can identify champions in each city and empower them to be your ambassadors. With a modest budget for pizza and drinks and an ambassador volunteering space and time each month, your program can scale cost-effectively.

At Gainsight, we took our brand for our big event (Pulse—more on this below) and created Pulse Local, where customer success champions in dozens of cities host local meetups about customer success in their offices. This creates the organic conversation that truly drives community and trust.

Elevate: Intimate Executive Events

While we started big with our annual Pulse conference in 2013, we eventually decided to go smaller. In 2015, we launched CCO Summit, now called Pulse CXO.

The concept at the time was inspired by a group Nick is in— Young Presidents' Organization (YPO). YPO is a worldwide association where local groups of CEOs get together once a month in a confidential and candid setting to share openly. For Nick, YPO is the most transformative development activity he's done in his career. So Nick and Anthony Kennada (our chief marketing officer at the time) wondered, "Is there a version of this we could offer to chief customer officers?"

As they say, "It's lonely at the top." This is true for CEOs but it's probably also true for whatever executive stakeholder or decision-maker you sell to. In our case, CCOs were in a new role. Their charters weren't yet well defined. Their companies didn't always understand what they did. Neither did their families. And most importantly, they often felt alone.

We launched CCO Summit as an experiment—to bring the spirit of YPO to CCOs. We partnered with a facilitator Nick knew from YPO (Kaley Klemp) and brought approximately 50 CCOs together for the first summit in Menlo Park, California. The idea was to make it an "unconference."

Over the one-and-a-half-day agenda, we had merely two hours of "main stage" content to set the tone. The rest of the time was Warner and a set of other facilitators running carefully selected groups of six to eight CCOs discussing topics they were all wrestling with—org structures, compensation, budgeting, and the like. None of it was related to Gainsight. But all of it built trust and community.

Speaking of community, over the years we have tried to bring our company value of childlike joy to these events, including:

- A for-charity mini-golf obstacle course contest (you had to be there)
- A painting activity
- Trust-building exercises
- Group meditation

If your reaction is "My customers would never do that," we thought so too beforehand. But bringing human-first spirit to these events transformed them from corporate conferences into something much more. As proof, we have run this event every year since 2015 (barring a brief intermission for COVID). After each event, we use the NetPromoter System to rate the event. We have received a 90 or higher NPS for every single event, which is beyond world-class. We'd attribute the vast majority of this to the spirit and vibe of this series.

Scale: Roadshows

Sometimes you have an idea so good that you have to take it on the road. Community-building works in one-off dinners and events, but sometimes a series can galvanize a community around change. Road-shows are a powerful way to scale your events strategy by finding a theme or topic that the community is passionate about and spreading it across your geographic target markets. In theory, road shows are simple—they are a series of events. But in practice, the details matter.

We've run many roadshow series over the years, but the one Nick is proudest of probably includes some bias. In 2023, Taylor Swift started her Eras Concert Tour. As an homage, Gainsight's creative field events team created the Gainsight ERAS Tour, with ERAS standing for expansion, retention, adoption, and success, four priorities for most customer success leaders. ERAS for Gainsight became a way to rally the customer success community around the latest themes in the field in a playful and timely theme.

Some learnings from our experiences over the years:

- Just as with other events, the main value proposition is networking. As such, market the opportunity to meet peers on the same journey and build space into the agenda to make that a reality. For us, that meant ample time before the main content and afterward to discuss.
- On that note, we think of content as merely a teaser to prompt discussion. Rather than having three hours of presentations, we opted for a three-hour event with less than one hour of content.
- Each city and country may differ, but we've found that a late breakfast often represents a lower commitment and tradeoff for clients than a dinner.
- Branding and childlike joy again create the atmosphere to foster openness.
- We encourage icebreakers and assigned seating to make sure dialogue emerges.

"The Big Daddy": Conferences

We saved this for last because the idea of putting on your own conference can seem intimidating. For us at Gainsight, it was kind of an accident.

When we launched our company in 2013, we served a brand-new job and field: customer success. We hosted a meetup in our office, catered with the cheapest grocery store wine and cheese our limited funding could buy. Despite the modest accoutrements, our 3000-square-foot workspace was flooded with people. The demand was off the charts for humans in this new profession to make connections.

As such, Anthony Kennada (our first CMO) and Nick said, "Let's run an event—for real." Our big goal was 100 people, and we rented out a small hotel ballroom in San Francisco for our first Pulse conference. When 300 people showed up and the fire marshal ended up having to intervene, we knew we were on to something.

Over the years, Pulse became a legendary event series and took its place as the defining industry event for the profession. Along the way, we've learned enough to write an entire separate book, but we'll share the shorthand below. You can find copious resources online about event planning generally, so we'll try to share 10 unique learnings we've had:

1. **What's in a name:** You might notice our event is called Pulse, not "Gainsight Conference." That was intentional. We wanted to separate our brand from the community. We wish we had a better story for picking the name Pulse (it just sounded cool), but the idea of a separate brand gave our audience a feeling that this was different from a "vendor conference."

2. **Community first, commercial second:** If you attend a typical vendor conference, you'll often see the CEO get up, welcome the audience, and quickly jump into a sales pitch. At Pulse, the welcome keynote is all about the customer success profession, including stats about its growth, the latest best practices, and even a fist bump between audience members to build connections. On that note, Nick always restates the purpose of Pulse—to create a community to help this profession connect with peers, be inspired, and feel a little bit less lonely.

3. **Community sourced:** Speaking of community, many vendor conference agendas are packed full of product-oriented content from the vendor and customers doing their own sales pitches for the vendor. In contrast, we ask the community to submit topics around the *job* of customer success. As such, the agenda over the years has covered

compensation, organizational structure, hiring, and many other topics that have nothing to do with our software.

4. **Maniacal content review:** At the same time, the Pulse event is ours so we need to ensure the standards are top-notch. We are very prescriptive with presenters. Make the intro about your company brief. Make the slides simple and visual. Leave time for Q&A. Bring humor and joy to the presentation. Make it interactive. Over the years, we've done everything from offering professional speaker training to presenters to literally having Nick review every session. To this day, Nick asks each presenter to make a two-minute video of their concept so he can provide feedback.

5. **Bring the energy:** It's not about what you say, it's how you say it. At the first Pulse, Nick walked on stage and asked, "Who's excited? Who's fired up?" Eventually, "Who's Fired Up?" became the unofficial motto for Pulse, eventually even turning into an original rap song about customer success under the same name. It's available on Spotify, and you can become the next person to stream it (the first nine were Nick's family)! But being "fired up" captures what we aspire to at Pulse. We want every presenter to bring energy on stage because energy is infectious. We try to amplify this with walk-on music and DJs. But the core is that if the company is fired up, the audience will be too.

6. **Leave space for networking:** That being said, one of the main reasons people are fired up about Pulse is to leave the audience and to go to the hallways. Over the years, Pulse has become a reunion for customer success professionals. As folks move around between jobs, it's a way for people to reconnect, as well as to build new relationships. The most important part is having an agenda with lots of breaks. But on top of that, we recommend structured activities like lunch tables with topics (so people self-select) or "birds of a feather" groups where clients can deep-dive with like-minded

attendees. In addition, event networking technology can help a great deal in this regard.

7. **Charge to force yourself to deliver value:** We have always charged attendees for Pulse. The idea was that this is *not* a vendor event. People get professional value from the conference, so they should be willing to pay. This forced us to truly deliver on the value. In addition, it allowed us to have the budget to fund an incredible show.

8. **Logistics matter:** While we said we won't cover it here, the only low points at Pulse have been the downfalls of every conference—short on coffee, registration breakdowns, and temperature malfunctions. It's all very solvable, but this is where your event staff is absolutely mission critical to success.

9. **Childlike joy FTW:** And now for the most unique part about Pulse. We always channel our value of childlike joy at the event. This creates a spirit of camaraderie that captures the essence of community. Over the years, this has shown up in various ways:

   - Our rap song performed on stage by Nick (the beginning and end of his rap career)
   - A '90s-themed event with a set based upon "Central Perk" from the TV show *Friends*
   - A party on an aircraft carrier
   - A surprise performance by Vanilla Ice (You know which song he performed....)
   - Countless parody videos, channeling Taylor Swift, *Ted Lasso*, Garth Brooks, Disney, and more

10. **Vulnerability deepens connections:** In Nick's intro, he tries to guide the audience to let down their guard and be real. Everyone is struggling, and no one is perfect. To foster this, in his closing, he has chosen a topic each year to get vulnerable about—with thousands of his closest acquaintances. He has openly talked about loneliness as a child, depression, his father's dementia, his sadness about his daughter growing up and

graduating, and more. Brené Brown taught us that vulnerability can be our greatest strength, which has shown up at Pulse.

As mentioned, we could write a separate book on Pulse and all our offline events. But we hope with this chapter, we inspired you on the value of offline events and gave you some pointers to start building events or bring them to the next level.

And online and offline strengthen each other from a conceptual perspective as well as from a practical perspective. After all, how do you promote your event and register attendees? And where do you afterward share your after-movie and the valuable content? Indeed, that's mostly done online. While many of those experiences are still fragmented, we want to encourage you to bring them together in your customer hub. And that's what we will discuss in the next chapter.

12

Law 8: Tie It All Together in One Customer Hub

Prevent a Disjointed Customer Experience by Integrating Engagement and Content

By Alistair Field, Cristina Rotariu, and Sebastiaan Terpstra

Let's say you're a user of Logo Ipsum, a fictional B2B company that offers a suite of marketing products. You're trying to figure out how to set up an email campaign to onboard new customers, but you get stuck because you don't know where to start, nor do you have any concrete examples as to what constitutes a good onboarding campaign.

You decide to check out the knowledge base, which you discovered through a link in the product. Running a quick search lands you on the support article that outlines how to build your first email campaign. Great! However, knowing how to filter an audience and set up some rules is one thing. Knowing how to build a good campaign is another.

So you decide to Google. Apparently there's also a thriving online community for Logo Ipsum that has a dedicated category for sharing best practices around email campaigns. Searching a bit further, you land on the Logo Ipsum blog, where Logo Ipsum shared an article called "Three Examples of Great Email Campaigns." In the blog's sidebar you see a link to Logo Ipsum's events portal, and—what a coincidence—there's an upcoming webinar with a tutorial on how to build awesome campaigns.

Because you know how much product teams value feedback, you decide to also share an idea for Logo Ipsum in their external ideas portal to offer a set of flywheel email campaigns so that future customers can hit the ground running. A few months later you receive an email from Logo Ipsum's (product) marketing team that they've implemented your idea. How cool!

As you can imagine, this is not a realistic scenario for a few reasons. First, most customers aren't as persistent as the one in this story. They may reach out to your customer support team or their customer success manager to get their questions answered. For one, this adds an additional obstacle for your customers to be successful while also increasing the workload of your customer-facing teams, which makes it harder for you to scale. At worst, customers may have given up on exploring and using that feature altogether.

Second, apart from being persistent, you were lucky to discover that there was such a wide, albeit scattered, offering of customer success resources such as an online community, an inspirational blog, an events section, an ideas portal, and even a product update newsletter. And Logo Ipsum was lucky that your Google search led you to *their* resources on creating great campaigns, and not one of Logo Ipsum's competitors' resources. Even if you work to tie your customer success resources together as best as you can, it still creates a fractured customer journey that's far from ideal.

Danny Pancratz, director of community at Unqork, captured this well: "Very quickly, the number of resources that a creator, a customer, or partner might have bookmarked grew to be over 10. In the feedback collected through NPS and CSAT, we learned that our resources were great, but people were struggling to find them or know what to use."

Now let's look at it from the other side of the coin. You work for Logo Ipsum, and you're in charge of the customer experience. Traditionally, you've got a knowledge base in (e.g., Zendesk or Intercom) where your customers can find how-to articles on specific features and integrations. Because Logo Ipsum has a strong maker audience, you've launched an online community for your makers to share ideas and ask questions. Because Logo Ipsum is seen as a thought leader, your marketing team invests heavily in creating helpful and inspirational content they share on your blog. Your CS team wants to actively share best practices with their customers, so they host a recurring webinar series where peers share their best practices that they promote on a dedicated events page. Your product team uses a dedicated tool to capture ideas from your customers to inform the roadmap and relies on your marketing department to ensure that their feature updates reach your customers' inboxes.

Sound familiar? The fact that your company provides this breadth and depth to ensure your customers are successful means that your company recognizes the importance of customer success. This drive, in fact, is engrained in all of your customer-facing teams. However, the content is siloed, not orchestrated, and is likely dependent on each of Logo Ipsum's teams if, when, and how it reaches your customer.

Just as in the example above, for customers to know and leverage the full breadth of customer success content requires an unlikely amount of persistence on their end to discover that there's more than only knowledge base articles to help them out. This means that in most cases, customers most likely just fall back on one-to-one support, or it leads to customers simply giving up.

Also, from Logo Ipsum's end, it requires either a lot of luck or some serious complex journey orchestration for your customers to realize that there is such a comprehensive offering of customer success resources such as an online community, an inspirational blog, an events section, an ideas portal, and even a product update newsletter. This still creates a fractured customer journey that leaves a good amount of potential untapped. Most companies we have seen experienced this challenge. And then we haven't even touched upon the disjointed data and analytics layer this causes across systems.

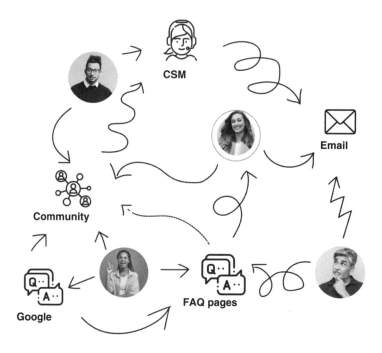

- Existing content is fragmented and not reaching customers.
- Most customer engagement is high-touch, with email as the main channel.
- The customer journey is highly fragmented.

Silos and Misalignment

Irrespective of the quality of the content created, as long as it lives and is presented in siloes, it will create a fragmented journey that requires a healthy dose of persistence and luck for it to reach its full potential. Furthermore, through this approach, we not only compromise the potential for a customer's success, we also adversely affect the way teams work together internally.

Maybe you recognize some of the following situations:

- The marketing team just released a newsletter, but wasn't aware of recent product releases from the product team that they could have included.
- The customer success manager just told a customer that we would not invest in feature X in the short term, while the product team is talking to the same customers, doing discovery for feature X.
- The support team has to give a lot of support on a certain feature caused by bad UX that may be blocking adoption, but the product team has never heard of that issue through the product feedback channel.
- The product team wants to send out a product updates newsletter, while the marketing team is already sending out a generic newsletter that has no room for it.

It's likely that each department will eventually communicate with *the same* customer or communicate something probably limited to that department's domain only (e.g., product feedback, product support, customer education, events, etc.). Not only can this lead to friction internally (e.g., two departments sending mixed messages about a release date, or feedback being interpreted differently by two teams), but it also leads to knowledge and context living in silos that prevent your teams from being able to tap into insights, contribute to the customer experience, and monitor customer behavior.

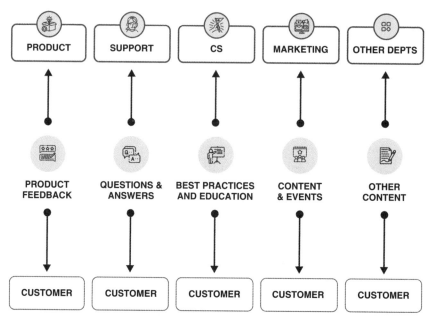

Siloed customer communications

Bringing It All Together

So far we've established that customers need to be both persistent and lucky to find the resources that they need (which they typically aren't), and that internal teams, all with good intentions, are still misaligned and miss necessary context from other teams. This leaves a big opportunity on the table to make your customer's success less reliant on persistence and luck, and to increase internal alignment around the voice of the customer.

Let's talk about the customer's perspective first. To retain customers, it's paramount to make your customers successful in increasing satisfaction and preventing churn. To make your customer's success less dependent on persistence and luck, it's important to take charge on their behalf and ensure that you centralize all customer success content and engagement in one central location. This will allow your customers to find answers to their questions in one place, regardless of whether it's answered by another user, a knowledge base article, a blog, a product update, or the like. And if they can't find it, sharing your question in the one place where all your customers come together will significantly increase the odds of their question being answered by a peer.

The scattered journey needs to be replaced with a centralized experience for end users to increase findability of content, lower customer effort scores, and offer a seamless experience.

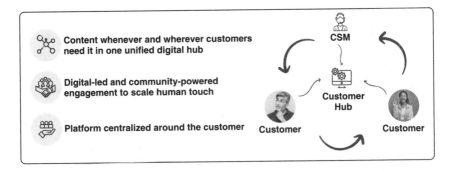

Talking about the internal perspective, leveraging a centralized customer hub used by multiple teams across the organization allows these teams to work and share knowledge across functional silos. Moreover, this will set up your customer-facing teams to tap into the same source of customer insights, collaborate on the customer experience, and keep a pulse on customer sentiment.

Instead of siloed customer communication, we bring it all together in one central hub.

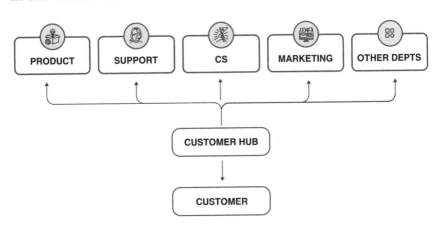

Building a customer hub Tied to the Customer Journey

In 2013, Scott Hudgins, current chief commercial officer at Walt Disney World, said, "Nobody owns the customer, but someone always owns the moment" (Williams, 2022). In the context of Walt Disney World, that moment is the purchase of the ticket, the welcome into the park, the ride operators, the character performers, the food service, and more. Each one of these interactions is person-to-person and face-to-face.

For a SaaS product or company, the customer engages with the sales team prior to purchase, then an onboarding or education team, a support team, a customer success team, and maybe even a product services team, before a renewals team at the end of the initial contract. That is a large number of moments giving rise to the risk of inconsistent customer experience. As we've established above, bringing all those teams together in one centralized hub can reduce that risk and provide an seamless experience.

We will explore the building blocks of a customer Hub and touch on how they relate to each stage of the customer journey.

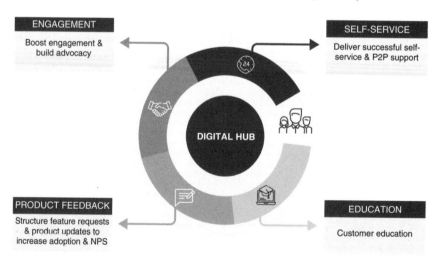

Each component of the Hub contributes to the customer's experience at every stage of the customer journey, as we discussed in Law 3.

Prospective Customers

Consumers research and investigate a product and company before making a purchase. Offering these prospects a place for discussions in your hub allows you to market your post-sales experience in the early phases. Hosting discussions provides the opportunity for you to give advocates a place to share experiences with your company and is a clear sign to the customer of transparency and collaboration.

Onboarding

Post-launch, activities are often repetitive. They help bring the customer up to speed on your product. This is a fantastic opportunity to promote engagement in your hub by providing access to training materials, centralizing all onboarding content, and encouraging self-service. The customer Hub acts as the central place for new users to get familiar with your products.

Adoption and Maturity

As customers mature, their knowledge and connection to the product will deepen. Having been encouraged to consume in earlier stages of their customer life, they now feel empowered to contribute and make their voice heard in the platform—for example, on product ideation and feedback. This is how you find and groom your advocates.

Every year, Salesforce researches and reports on the State of the Connected Customer. The results from the report clearly indicate we are entering a trust-based economy. More than 88% of customers believe trust becomes more important in times of change, and 96% of customers say excellent customer service builds trust (Salesforce, 2022). The building blocks of a customer Hub bring the company and customer departments closer together to provide that experience and build that trust.

Improving Self-Service with a Customer Hub

The benefits of self-service are well documented and accepted on both the vendor and user sides. For the vendor, successful self-service equates to lower support costs, faster time to proficiency, and better employee engagement as they are working on the "harder" problems and there is feedback on the content they present.

There is also significant value to be obtained by understanding the behaviors of your customers within the Hub. You can move beyond the content of questions in support tickets to track what questions are asked in the community, what searches are occurring through the hub, and, ultimately, what content is missing or underperforming.

Furthermore, having a robust methodology for creating and maintaining knowledge is paramount to success. One such methodology is Knowledge-Centered Service® (KCS), a widely adopted methodology established by the Consortium for Service Innovation. It offers value to organizations and communities by making knowledge abundant and available so that problems can be solved. KCS provides a framework for demand-driven content creation. That is, content is created at the time of need instead of preemptively looking to provide solutions to problems that have not materialized in the customer base. This is where a Customer Hub activity can give a real insight into the needs of your users and guide content creation. Similarly, useful solutions and content provided by customers in the community that prove popular can be converted to official documentation and maintained as part of the company's knowledge resources moving forward.

By combining multiple types of content—like community Q&A, knowledge base articles, educational content, and more—into one single destination, companies can overcome the traditional content silo. Customers can be tracked across all activities versus in disparate systems and locations. Content can be moved, merged, and extended more easily, and the user experience flourishes.

Centralizing Engagement in the Customer Hub

The Customer Hub is built of many pillars of needs for the customer as they progress through their journey with your product. If we could summarize these moments with one word, it would be *connection*—to the right information and to the right person.

That person may or may not be an internal employee. The right person is the person who has the right response at the right time. Only via deploying a centralized hub where customers, employees, and partners engage can they constructively help each other in their time of need, increasing connection.

Customer Hub Supports the Full Product Management Workflow

In her book, *Continuous Discovery Habits,* Teresa Torres (2021) talks about how product teams "are collectively responsible for ensuring that their products create value for the customer in a way that creates value for the business." As straightforward and widely accepted as this statement is, it is equally difficult to put this into practice and conduct day-to-day product work closely following this recipe, for two main reasons.

Firstly, *value for customers* can take many forms, even when addressing the same customer needs, and can be formulated in many different ways depending on how many customers you talk to. Furthermore, any company's goal is constantly increasing its customer base, but expecting product teams to converse with this ever-growing number of people is unrealistic. Because of this, product people fall into the trap of listening to the loudest voice threatening to churn, the highest-paying customers, or the most impressive logo. The rationale is if these people have their needs met and get the desired value, it will be the same for the rest of their product users.

Secondly, though equally important as the first reason, quantifying or predicting the *value for business* is often a game of estimation. Predictions for retention metrics and sales conversion rates are closely related to how much certainty is being given by the *value delivered to customers.* However, from hearing a customer's pain point or need to delivering a solution that potentially and hopefully addresses it, the road has many twists and turns. How can product teams optimize their journey to create a symbiotic relationship between customer value and business value?

There is no magic spell or crystal ball, but a customer hub can significantly alleviate the unknowns and pains of having comprehensive discovery, solution validation, beta testing efforts, release announcements, and adoption-driving challenges. Customers are invited to ask and answer each other's product-related questions, and easily learn how to leverage existing product capabilities more efficiently. Once they encounter product limitations, they can quickly raise their needs by submitting ideas and product requests that arrive directly under the product team's eyes. Furthermore, on an ideation board, customers often challenge each other when raising product requests and complement each other's use cases, which otherwise would fall solely on the shoulders of a product manager in their one-to-one conversation with a customer. We all know how tricky this conversation can turn out to be—a product manager has to sound either too difficult by probing customers with lots of questions, too cryptic not to give away solution biases they might have, or too accepting of the proposals they hear, risking creating unrealistic expectations with their users. When these conversations are happening in the open, on an idea thread, the product managers get to be a moderator of a constructive discussion, with less risk of needing to play either the bad or the good cop.

Additionally, the need to identify the popular ideas and product requests that will deliver value to most customers is solved through the voting system. It is no longer the game of the loudest voice but a more democratic process capturing a more realistic image of the customers' needs and, implicitly, the value they desire from the product. These ideas capture a more holistic list of acceptance criteria and must-haves, helping the product teams discover with more confidence solutions that are on the right path to satisfying the customer and delivering company value.

Anita Hæhre, Senior Director Community at Cognite, best highlighted the benefits of opening the customer hub to product discussions: "Gathering ideas on the hub has allowed us to understand the power of customer feedback at scale, and access those insights in seconds."

Closing the Loop

In the early days, Gainsight turned to community as a solution to channel the product feedback received from customers via CSMs and support teams. We decided that its primary function would be to serve as the heart of the product feedback loop, and ultimately to close that loop.

Denise Stokowski, group VP of platform products at Gainsight, explains this approach: "The goal is to provide a forum for customers, partners, and Gainsight employees to provide product feedback that impacts the roadmap and to receive product support and solutions from peers."

Once the product team has drawn up a product solution to a customer need, the hub offers an easy way to communicate it back to all those interested in it, keeping them informed about the progress made and involving them further in the validation process. This kind of communication enables quick validation and learning cycles, increasing the confidence of both the product team that they are working on the right thing and of the customers that they have been heard and a solution is on its way. Tools focused solely on gathering and organizing product feedback do not cover communicating back to customers unless via intermediaries like CSMs. When the time comes to test a solution within a beta program, the customer hub is again the perfect stage to draw in volunteers, keep communication away from everyone's already overloaded inboxes, and maintain transparency for everyone involved. Furthermore, product teams can ensure that they have a balanced pool of customers in their beta programs to gain the most out of the beta and create experts in that new functionality who can help others later on.

A new feature delivers its value when customers are informed about it, are educated on how to use it, and are using it successfully. The customer hub is again the perfect place for product teams and companies to announce their new releases, any change in their product, and their updated roadmaps. A release note and a knowledge base article on how to use the newly released feature will ensure a strong foundation for all adoption-driving efforts. Existing and future customers will learn about a product's capabilities and best practices by having such content in one place. Apart from tracking success and adoption metrics, product teams would have the chance to gauge the immediate impact of their release by reading the customers' reactions and be able to act quickly on any questions or concerns raised by users.

According to Anita Hæhre from Cognite, "We've tapped into the core of our company's product lifecycle by working closely with product and engineering, driving early adopter programs and product ideation to ensure product-market fit. We're also working closely with our academy department for training and certifying, our documentation team, support, and managed services."

Finding a Balance

Should a company use ideas submitted to the community as the only input for their roadmaps and strategies? Definitely not! The product vision should remain the lighthouse guiding ideas into a safe harbor where the product strategy is the coast guard deciding which ideas and customer needs will make it onto the roadmap. Ideas can come from anywhere and everywhere, and customer interviews and one-to-one discussions should not be completely replaced by community ideation but should complement each other.

It remains imperative and valuable for product teams to have conversations with customers, for customer success managers to collect and share product feedback from their customer interactions, for support teams to share their insights from issues raised by customers in their tickets, and nevertheless for sales teams to gather insights from the market and potential customers to help product teams in keeping their product strategies relevant in creating business value for the company. Centralizing all these avenues into the hub is an ongoing process and a collective company-wide effort.

All-in-One Customer Education

We have touched on the importance of providing customers with materials to educate them about newly released functionality. Knowledge base articles are dedicated to providing helpful content to users to make the most out of the product's capabilities. However, customer education goes beyond knowledge base articles and helpful content. More than ever, companies should now strive to help customers better understand and gain more knowledge of the field they are acting in. For this reason, companies are creating courses that go beyond the usage of their product, touch upon best practices in that particular field, and aim to develop skills that are required to succeed. Creating thought leadership that continuously innovates and pushes the boundaries of what's possible and organizing webinars to enable the community to share their knowledge and experience fosters the "success for all" mentality.

Engagement flourishes when all these educational efforts find their home within a customer hub. Customers are not only helped with product questions and their day-to-day challenges but are also being empowered with courses and thought leadership content from the customer hub and are being supported in their professional development. Companies can reuse the content for different purposes. For example, in easy-to-follow onboarding flows, quick troubleshooting guides, and in-app education flows on functionalities. In addition, by providing valuable and holistic education, their relationships with their customers will be strengthened, gaining well-deserved advocates and achieving their goals around retention rates.

Customer Hub in Your Tech Stack

Every company has its own unique DNA and specific needs for which they have carefully selected different vendors and solutions to ensure their optimal operation. While a customer hub can help with centralizing a large part of customer-facing communication, it can also serve as a way to limit the number of company vendors used. By centralizing different technologies like communities, knowledge base, customer education platforms, in-app engagements, advocacy tools, and product feedback tools in one central platform, not only does the customer experience improve, but also the total costs of ownership for your business will decrease.

The customer hub will act as a platform for your customers. It can be combined and integrated with more internal workflow and CRM systems. Data around a customer's engagement and sentiment of all interactions are valuable and can provide actionable insights when shared and aggregated in a customer success platform.

The ultimate key to success is transitioning from one tool to another and making the user experience as seamless as possible without them noticing that the solution has changed in the background. In the end, customers' experiences shouldn't be fragmented by different authentication processes, needing to know about different channels and how to arrive on their own in another tool, or, worse, having to repeat their requests or questions. User journeys like escalating a ticket to the support team from the community, answering a support ticket with content from the hub, offering on the customer hub suggestions of courses to help a user to get more out of the product they're using, and so much more can be achieved by having your tech stack integrated and connected.

Similarly, for a company's departments, having data and insights into their customers' situation at their fingertips will help avoid duplication of work, misalignment, and miscommunication and will offer a greater understanding of a customer's needs while enabling valuable collaboration between different teams, ensuring that customers are successful with the products and services they're using.

By now, the benefits of consolidating all efforts in one place sound like the most promising path toward success and growing retention rates. But does this now mean that companies should immediately drop other solutions they are using for some of the use cases discussed here? No more separate learning management systems, or event management tools, knowledge base solutions or chats? Of course not! Nowadays, most of these technologies follow the API-first approach, meaning that with some development effort, the existing tools in your tech stack can be integrated, letting data flow between them, and workflows are connected across platforms. However, a single integrated platform will likely achieve the best possible solution.

Looking Ahead

Throughout this book, we have seen that the customer hub is much more than just a self-service tool to minimize support cases and scale your service offering. The customer hub will become a data-driven, personalized, and orchestrated journey for your customer base, completely integrated in your core product experience.

Through the hub, you will have a 360-degree view of what your customers are doing or not doing, their needs, and how your resources can best assist them. This can be fed back via integrations into your CS or CRM systems for account health purposes. Utilizing AI as the next step, the journey can be personalized at each touch point through the behavioral learnings of similar contractual users and inputs from each integrated system. For the customer, the seamless integration of knowledge, training, support, and product guidance will minimize effort, reduce time to value, and provide experiences that keep them coming back for more.

The customer hub of the future will be the focal point for any CS program, whether one-to-many or white-glove-enterprise level. It will be a highly personalized digital data-driven offering that gives your customer everything they need, where and when they need it.

13

Law 9: Community Should Drive Real Business Outcomes

Don't Get Fooled by Vanity Metrics—Demand Real Business Metrics

By Bas van Leeuwen, Valerie Molina, and Kenneth Refsgaard

It might seem obvious that a community program should drive tangible business outcomes. But that has not always been the case in the community space. As Erica Kuhl, an early community pioneer at Salesforce.com, told us, "I think not enough people in our industry are doing this; they're not yet speaking the language of business. We can't be talking about community the way we think about it because nobody understands it or necessarily cares. But if you speak to the business about their needs and what they will get in return—that gets that organization on board. Speak in dollars and cents. Speak in ROI. The most successful communities have done that well."

In the first wave of enterprise communities we described at the beginning of this book, the value was almost always based on cost reduction through the deflection of support tickets. As the use cases for community have expanded in recent years, we have seen various approaches emerge when considering what business outcomes a community is contributing to. In our experience, most companies with a community program soon find themselves in one of the following three scenarios:

- **Intrinsic belief in the value of community.** In some organizations, there is a genuine and innate belief that engaging with customers and investing in community programs is highly valuable, if not essential, for running their business. We see this most often with recently established companies where there is an understanding and appreciation of community at the founder and executive level. The community program may be part of the earliest business plans for the company and an essential element of the digital journey.

  In companies like these, there may never be a question of needing to directly measure the business value of the community. As Chris Petros, CMO at ServiceTitan, told us, "I see customer engagement as foundational. You can argue that breathing has an ROI at some level. You get to live another minute. Similarly, if you're not engaging with customers and understanding their needs, you're dead in the water."

  This might be similar to investing in a CRM system every year for which optimization work is a priority but few questions are ever raised about the necessity of having one. When asked about their business outcome metrics recently, a customer of ours told us, "We never get asked about value—that's a given in our organization." From a community practitioner's point of view, encountering this intrinsic trust is wonderful. However, it also brings risk, because a change in leadership, culture, or market status can leave the program in a precarious position.

- **Value is important but ROI is elusive.** The second scenario we often encounter is one where there is a desire to demonstrate the value that the community is delivering. Still, for various reasons, it is difficult to prove it. In a situation like this, the community team will probably focus on the proof points that are easiest to measure, such as cost reduction through support ticket deflection, for which there are well-established best practices such as customer surveys. That is a fantastic proof point, but a next-generation customer community has likely been set up with much greater ambition in mind across various use cases. Engaging with customers at scale is critical in delivering on retention, adoption, and growth objectives. If the community team cannot directly correlate community value to these outcomes, they will likely focus on top-level measures of community engagement. This might be MAC (monthly active customers) or simply the number of visitors. We highly recommend MAC as an engagement measure, because it is a powerful indicator of the program's success. However, it still doesn't tell us what impact the community ultimately has on business outcomes. In our experience, most companies with community programs are currently in this situation.

- **The community program drives proven quantifiable business outcomes.** This situation is currently the least common, taking us right to the leading edge of where communities are evolving. Not many companies have yet matured and operationalized their community programs to the level where business value is proven or strongly correlated. Nevertheless, we strongly believe that communities directly contribute to retention and growth outcomes, and we would encourage every community leader to work toward proving value in this way. This is the scenario we'd like more companies to discover for themselves.

A Reporting Framework Based on Value

Throughout the rest of this chapter, we will explore some of the most powerful ways we have found of measuring community value in correlation with bottom-line business goals. We hope this will help you design a scalable and long-term community strategy. It will help you build a solid business case as you're starting your program and securing initial investment, as well as help you develop and optimize your plan for the community over time.

As Daniel Quick, SVP of content strategy at Thought Industries, said at Gainsight's Pulse 2022 conference, "Without a focus on meaningful business results, even if you execute every other step of this measurement strategy to perfection, at the end of the day, you will have demonstrated . . . what?" (Quick, 2022).

We've found it helpful to frame business outcomes around the following four fundamental categories or value drivers:

- **Retention:** By providing your customers with helpful resources and a place to engage with your company and peers in a similar situation, you elevate their experience and make it more likely that they will maintain their relationship with your company and product.
- **Scale and efficiency:** The first generation of enterprise communities was about helping support organizations scale by deflecting tickets. For many companies, communities are essential for delivering efficiencies across the organization, particularly for delivering a digital customer success strategy.
- **User experience and product adoption:** Communities serve as centralized engagement hubs full of helpful content and best practices for your product. This directly reduces friction and increases product adoption.
- **Expansion:** Communities can effectively highlight product capabilities to drive expansion goals. That means generating more revenue through marketing, sales, cross-sells, and upsells.

It's helpful to identify your most important value drivers upfront to build a community program deeply tied to your company's needs. Which of the four value drivers is most important to your company and program?

Prioritizing Business Outcomes Over Outputs

Going one level deeper means taking the value drivers that are most important to you and then outlining the more specific business outcomes related to them, and not falling into the pitfall of only considering outputs. If you can identify what your organization is trying to achieve, you can directly identify how the community can support those needs. In an article for the *Harvard Business Review,* Jeff Gothelf and Josh Seidan (2017) write, "most teams in business work to create a defined output. But just because we've finished making a thing doesn't mean that thing is going to create economic value." The same logic applies to software and communities.

When you don't understand what your company is trying to achieve at the highest level, you'll continuously face uncertainty with your projects and initiatives. As Gothelf and Seidan put it, "the relationship between 'we've finished building it' and 'it has the effect we intended' is much less clear . . . this problem of uncertainty, combined with the nature of software, means that managing our projects in terms of outputs is simply not an effective strategy in the digital world. And yet our management culture and tools are set up to work in terms of outputs."

Next to outcomes that are already clearly defined as business priorities in the organization, there may also be themes where the community can drive impact but that haven't been fully identified before. This allows room for identifying new opportunities.

Also, demonstrating the business impact of a well-managed community will allow for a lot of freedom in operations. As long as goals are being achieved, there will be trust in the program.

Start from the Top and Work Your Way Down

To align your outcomes and value metrics with those of the wider business, we recommend starting at the top with the four value drivers mentioned. Any initiative that doesn't in some way contribute to one or more of these areas could, quite rightly, be questioned.

Here are some examples of outcomes that we often see successful companies focus on when building their community programs:

- **Scale and efficiency:** Increase self-service, prioritize R&D efficiently, and increase CSM efficiency.
- **User experience and product adoption:** Increase adoption, improve the customer journey, and improve customer experience.
- **Retention:** Increase health score predictiveness, reduce risk and churn, and improve renewal forecast accuracy.
- **Expansion:** Increase growth through advocacy, improve expansion pipeline, improve expansion velocity, and improve new business pipeline.

In our experience, the majority of companies building community programs are prioritizing the first two: scale and efficiency, and user experience and product adoption. Those areas are the most obvious starting points in many cases and have been discussed extensively throughout this book. Over time, however, as a community program matures, it's likely that there will be a greater focus on broader value drivers that relate directly to retention or expansion.

Leading and Lagging Indicators

Every company will have a set of high-level metrics that are seen as crucial indicators of the health of the business. These are likely to include hard financial figures, of course, but many of the companies we work with are focusing heavily on net revenue retention (NRR) and gross revenue retention (GRR) as these retention-focused metrics are increasingly proven to be among the most vital indicators of long-term growth. Another common top-level metric is net promoter score (NPS), which has historically been a strong indicator of long-term growth and business health.

Most companies also have a set of metrics for the value drivers that are seen as the most direct indicators of value and business health. We call these "lagging indicators," and they are the metrics we ultimately want to influence with all our initiatives, including our community program. They are called "lagging indicators" because their impact tends to lag behind the immediate efforts we make in our businesses. They are relatively tricky to impact directly and immediately. Nevertheless, we need to understand how our actions are influencing these top-level indicators, and one of the ways we do that is by identifying their most precise leading indicators. A "leading indicator" is a relatively easy metric to impact directly and immediately, where a strong case for attribution can be made toward one of the top-level "lagging indicators."

Let's look at an example for each of the four value drivers.

Scale and Efficiency		
Outcome	*Leading Indicators*	*Lagging Indicators*
Increase self-service	Views of helpful content % marked as best answers % of answers by peer	Decrease in support ticket volumes Decrease in cost-to-serve

User Experience and Product Adoption		
Outcome	*Leading Indicators*	*Lagging Indicators*
Improve adoption	Views of educational content webinar attendance rates	Product adoption (both width and depth)

Improve Retention		
Outcome	*Leading Indicators*	*Lagging Indicators*
Reduce churn risk	Monthly active customers (MAC)	NRR GRR

Increase Expansion		
Outcome	*Leading Indicators*	*Lagging Indicators*
Improve expansion pipeline	Community qualified leads (CQLs)	Pipeline growth NRR

By starting to report on community value in this way, with a focus on the top leading indicators that relate to the outcomes we are looking to influence in conjunction with the lagging indicators, we are building a strong case for long-term attribution of value from our community program initiatives. As we see in the preceding example, when we are looking to drive product adoption, we can start by tracking the engagement rates of all of our product-related community initiatives. Are we seeing growth in traffic toward content focused on product capabilities? Are customers increasingly attending our product-focused webinars? As we see and prove momentum and success with these community initiatives, any changes to actual product adoption can be partly attributed to the community program.

Calculating Direct Correlations

These four value drivers are a great starting point, and we typically recommend companies start by putting together a value framework. Working with leading and lagging indicators allows you to immediately start building a compelling story around the value the community is delivering. It is possible, however, to go further and start tracking direct correlations. This becomes increasingly essential for mature community programs that are discussed and evaluated at the C-level alongside other key business functions and programs.

In our experience, not many community teams do this effectively today, largely because calculating direct correlations has historically been technically challenging. It often takes combining disparate data sets in a way that requires effort from multiple teams and considerable technical know-how. However, the community space is seeing rapid innovation around data and integrations, so we expect these metrics to become standardized in the coming years. We see this particularly when a combination of a community and a customer success platform allows those data sets to be closely integrated in a way that natively surfaces valuable correlations. The customer hub we discussed in the previous law helps ensure aggregated data and a 360-degree view.

In the provided examples, we highlighted that we could take community engagement as a leading indicator (monthly active customers, or MAC) and use it to create a case for attribution toward improvement to retention metrics like NRR and GRR. This is a strong case, as we know that customer engagement is a key indicator of retention and is always represented at the heart of a good customer success strategy within the customer health scoring system. To go one step further, however, and calculate direct correlation, we can look at the community engagement of individual customers and correlate it with actual retention outcomes in the form of NRR or GRR. This will provide us with a correlation such as "Customers who are active community members have X% higher or lower NRR than nonactive community members." The same principle could be applied to any of the other outcomes—for example, "Customers who participate in our webinars have X% higher or lower product adoption," or "Customers who ask questions in our community are X% less or more likely to create more than two support tickets in a month."

Patrick Smith, CMO at Cvent, recently shared a great example when he told us, "When you have a big customer base, renewal rates are everything. So we do a lot of analysis around the leading indicators. We know that if organizations do certain things, their propensity to renew is higher, and one of those is being part of our community platform. So I don't get a lot of pushback from the CFO on why we're spending on this because everyone realizes how important renewal rates are. In a business of our scale, increasing your renewal rate by a couple of percentage points is a massive amount of money. And it's easier to keep a customer than to find a new one. So there's not one golden metric we look at, but there's no question that we're looking at community relative to the propensity to renew."

In addition to the examples provided, there is a well-established best practice for the self-service use case to calculate a correlation to support ticket deflection. This is often done with an online survey presented to community visitors, asking them if they had a question, whether they found their answer, and if they would have otherwise created a support ticket. The percentage of community members who answer yes to those three questions can then be applied to the total number of visitors to estimate deflected tickets. This is another strong indication of value.

Do all of these metrics prove causation? No, they don't. Arguably, when it comes to top-level value metrics like these, there is never such a thing as 100% certainty around causation. When a customer decides to renew or churn, is it because of the hard work of the CSM? Was it because of improvements to the product? Or was it because of the CS tool that was bought in the previous year? There are always multiple factors at play, but by gathering multiple strong indicators such as these, we can indicate the value that the community program is delivering in contributing to bottom-line value in a compelling way.

Community Health and Operational Metrics

At the beginning of this chapter, we outlined three situations that most community teams find themselves in. We mentioned that many community teams are focusing purely on operational metrics. The fact is that there are many metrics that community teams can (and in some cases should) be monitoring outside of the value-focused metrics we've discussed so far.

In particular, we always recommend monitoring what we call "community health." We look at community health as a small set of metrics that are excellent indicators of the underlying dynamics that power the community. For example, we might look at the percentage of visitors that convert to registration. Or the percentage of questions that get an answer. In a sense, these indicators suggest whether a community is successful and, therefore, likely to be adding value—but on their own they are not truly saying anything about value as such.

We see community health as a deeper layer of reporting that shows how well our community is functioning and provides clear and actionable direction to where and how to improve. This is important because this is where we might get some of the biggest insights into how we can influence our leading and lagging metrics. For example, suppose we are looking at MAC and NRR as leading and lagging indicators of retention. In that case, respectively, our community health framework might provide valuable insights into how we can drive higher MAC. For example, we might achieve this by improving the community experience to drive a higher conversion rate to registration.

The pitfall that we commonly see in the community space is to mix value, health, and other operational metrics. With the approach we have outlined, it's possible to clearly differentiate our value metrics from other metrics, which makes the story we tell much stronger and clearer.

Proving Value Drives Executive Buy-in

A successful community program has broad organizational buy-in, and the key to achieving that buy-in is to visibly contribute to key business outcomes.

As Mary Poppen, customer intelligence strategist and board advisor at Involve.ai, told us, "At the end of the day, everybody wants to know how it comes back to revenue. I had some people on my team run an analysis on upsell and renewal against community engagement. What was so interesting was that if at least one employee at a customer's company was active monthly in the community, they were eight times more likely to renew than a customer without engagement in our community. And there was a 13 times greater likelihood to expand revenue if they came to at least one of our VIP events in a year. That type of correlational analysis is huge in determining where you prioritize your investments and what's really strategic and important. That's how you get CEOs to say, 'This is strategic and important.'"

Every community is unique, and there isn't a one-size-fits-all approach to the metrics you should use to prove value. We hope that by using the guidance in this chapter, you'll be able to identify and prioritize the value drivers and outcomes that are important to your organization and put together a strong case for value using leading and lagging indicators and direct correlations.

At the end of the day, while the metrics are crucial, they're not the whole story. In Law 1, we discussed all the small ways to build authentic human connections with and among our customers. Since then, we've covered many of the most critical themes related to creating successful community engagement. Now it's time for us to circle back for our final law in this part of the book and focus on how we can bring our culture and values to our communities.

14 | Law 10: Bring Your Culture and Values to Your Community

Build with a Human-First Mindset

By Nick Mehta

April 10, 2018, was a big day in our company's history and an even bigger one in Nick's life. That Tuesday morning in San Mateo, California, at our Pulse conference marked the beginning of his unlikely rap music career. And a few minutes later, that day also coincided with its end.

The lineage of the one-hit customer success software wonder hip hop tribute, "Who's Fired Up?" started with a throwaway line from Nick's Pulse keynote five years earlier in 2013. To engage the audience in the first-ever Pulse conference, Nick opened the event with his eventual catchphrase: "Who's excited? Who's fired up?" Little did he know that that statement would become a mantra for the energy of the Pulse community. Over the years, Nick would open every event with the same cliched welcome to raucous enthusiasm from attendees. Eventually, Nick and Gainsight's former chief marketing officer, Anthony Kennada, had the idea to playfully turn the meme into a parody rap song about customer success, so "Who's Fired Up?" appeared on Spotify and YouTube.

While this certainly sounds like a plot from the satirical HBO TV show *Silicon Valley*, this story captures something more fundamental about communities: the most successful ones enable the attendees and organizers to be their true selves, quirks and all. At Gainsight, we coined the term "Human-First" to capture this spirit. The best communities have a truly human culture at their core.

But before we dive into community culture, let's start with company culture.

Company Culture

Culture as a concept parallels the ascent of human beings into societies. The *Oxford English Dictionary* definition of the term shows how broad and all-encompassing it is: "the customs and beliefs, art, way of life, and social organization of a particular country or group." The concept of company culture goes back to Elliott Jaques, who first introduced the concept of culture in the organizational context in his 1951 book *The Changing Culture of a Factory*. The book was a case study of the description, analysis, and development of corporate group behaviors in early factory organizations.

In today's business world, company culture has become a critical tool for recruiting, motivating, and retaining people in this increasingly competitive talent market. While many companies pay lip service to the concept, leading businesses authentically use culture as a competitive advantage.

Consider Netflix, one of the pioneers of modern and empowering employee culture. Netflix's approach, often captured in the terms

"Freedom and Responsibility" and canonized in a book of the same name, took Silicon Valley by storm when it came out. The Netflix "culture deck," a 128-slide presentation on its approach, provoked leaders to think differently. Instead of trying to fit in, Netflix's culture deck stood out for how it took a stand and looked different. Reed Hastings, Netflix co-founder and CEO for over 20 years, believed deeply in enabling teammates with as much autonomy as possible. So they embraced radical-sounding ideas like:

■ Giving unlimited vacation to employees, which was novel at the time
■ Letting employees make purchases without approvals
■ Encouraging aggressive performance management, such that "adequate performers" were moved out of the business quickly

Not every CEO or company agreed with Netflix's approach. And this is what made it brilliant. Netflix didn't create a culture for everyone. They made one that authentically fit their own needs and team. If you want to learn more about the Netflix culture, we highly recommend the book *No Rules Rules: Netflix and the Culture of Reinvention* by Reed Hastings and Erin Meyer.

Other highly respected organizations similarly leaned forward in defining their cultures:

■ HubSpot's "Culture Code" focused on their shared passion for their mission and metrics. The founders realized that whether you like it or not, you're going to have a culture, so why not make it one you love?
■ Salesforce made their value of trust central to everything they do and acknowledged that building this culture of trust is their greatest competitive advantage and differentiator.
■ It's no secret that Google has a different take on culture than the classic corporate work environment. Take a look at the Googleplex—that is the clearest evidence of a different culture!

What all strong company cultures have in common is that they are unique. And these culture trendsetters all extend their same spirit to their external stakeholders.

At Gainsight, it's our mission to be living proof that you can win at business while being Human-First. Our values guide our day-to-day work and orient all of us around this mission. Our values are guideposts on our quest to be a Human-First company—they're the perspective that we use every day to ensure we're on the right path as a company.

Here's a look at our five values:

- **Golden Rule:** We believe in treating people the way they want to be treated.
- **Success for All:** We believe in the tireless pursuit of balancing success for our customers, teammates, families, and community.
- **Childlike Joy:** We believe in bringing the inner child in us to work every day.
- **Shoshin:** We believe in a beginner's mind.
- **Stay Thirsty:** We believe in a totally internally driven striving for greatness.

These values mean a lot to us at Gainsight, and they're put into action through some incredible programs. That's why we are extra proud to be recognized as the winner of the annual Glassdoor Employees' Choice Awards, a list of the Best Places to Work in 2023. Unlike other workplace awards, there's no self-nomination or application process. Instead, it's entirely based on the feedback our teammates have voluntarily and anonymously shared on Glassdoor. Winning this award is a great validation of our mission and culture.

Breaking the Walls: Company Culture = Brand = Community Culture

As we mentioned in Chapter 1, the classic approach to business could best be captured by the iconic line from *The Godfather*, when leading character and Mafia boss Michael Corleone said, "It's not personal, it's strictly business." We'd argue that the strongest community cultures feel deeply personal.

Rather than retaining walls to separate how teammates operate at home, how they show up as employees, and how they interact with customers and other external stakeholders, the strongest communities "break the walls" and integrate their company culture with that of their community. The same principles and values that show up inside their physical or virtual office are the ones that connect their community together. This allows all community participants to be their true, Human-First selves.

As evidence of the importance of culture in communities, the State of Community Management report from the Community Roundtable (2022), the organization shared the "Culture Competency" of the Community Maturity Model, defined as "Habits, motivators (intrinsic and extrinsic), social norms, communications, decision-making processes, development processes, and learning approaches in an organization and/or community."

Increasingly, this transparency extends to the company's brand. As consumers and businesspeople, we've become cynical about businesses where their external persona is so different from their internal behaviors. We look to do business with companies that share our ideals and stand for what we do. As such, the inevitable trend is that internal company culture, community culture, and brand are one integrated whole.

Erica Kuhl launched Salesforce's community back in 2006. Here's what she says about culture in community:

> Culture is something that starts at the very beginning—the first person building it is the most important person to the future of the community because they influence that culture from the very beginning. I'm not saying that I was the be-all, end-all from a Trailblazer perspective, but I'm quirky and interested and curious, and I care deeply about what motivates people and why they do what they do. And I don't take myself so seriously, but I'm also serious in that I want the best for people. And so I think it's no

surprise that's why that community is far more than just enterprise software. Why it's really about people getting value, turning around, and bringing value to others. So for me, it's extremely important to never forget that there are people behind everything you do and to fully overemphasize what you're giving them before you expect to get anything.

Principles of Community Culture

What do you need to think about when defining your culture—whether it's for your company, for your community, or ideally both? Having run one of the most innovative communities in business and having studied many other successful networks, we posit there are five steps that are important in creating a strong community culture:

1. Define your values: what is common about your tribe
2. Determine what your community stands for
3. Identify and embrace your community's authentic quirks
4. Build a brand and voice for your community
5. Use vulnerability to open people up

Let's dig into the details.

Define Your Values: What Is Common About Your Tribe

We start out with the notion of "tribe," because we feel it captures the kindred spirit that defines a community. Something unites your community together. You just have to define what that is.

We'd argue that often the commonality is some deep emotion. As an example, let's talk about loneliness. We shared our personal stories of loneliness as children, which attracted us to this concept of community. In Gainsight's Pulse community, one of the most frequent emotions of attendees is that they feel alone in their day-to-day jobs in their companies and feel seen and a sense of belonging when they are together at Pulse. They are with people who "get them" and can finally commiserate on the highs and lows of the job. And because of this, the Pulse community is incredibly helpful to each other—as a sounding board or simply a shoulder to cry on.

Some ways we reinforce the desired behaviors include:

- Starting every Pulse event by defining these values around loneliness and connection and sharing examples from the past on how they have shown up
- Creating a ritual of the "Pulse fist bump" to have each attendee show their neighbor they are there for them
- Launching a job board and weekly job posting online to help the Pulse community find their next roles

But loneliness and connection are only two possible feelings that can be the glue for your community. Maybe your community is built on freedom or empowerment. Maybe it's all about innovation and creativity. Or perhaps your community is about rap videos—you never know.

Chris Petros, chief marketing officer of ServiceTitan, shared with us how his community has truly developed a culture. ServiceTitan builds software to serve "trades" professionals like plumbers and electricians. And they host a rocking event every year for their community called Pantheon:

> I think there's a couple of things that are very interesting that I've observed over the years. One is there's a very big sense of pride in being an entrepreneur. I think there's this feeling that people don't broadly necessarily recognize that, but there are tycoons in this industry that are flying private jets and doing billions in total value of sales. It's insane. I really have come to respect them as business people. If you go to Pantheon, and you see some of the contractors that are really hot in the trades and are doing things that are new or unique or inventive, you can't see one of them walk through the lobby of the hotel without 50 handshakes, introductions, questions, people glomming on to understand what they're doing. It's actually also very unique in that they stop and talk to everybody and help everybody and give everybody pointers.

Andrew Watts, chief customer officer at e-discovery leader Relativity, sees a unique vision in his community:

> I would say our community culture is inventive. At our Relativity Fest conference, the community participants vote on which of their peers were the most innovative in the last year. They get really excited about this.

Similarly, Elissa Fink, former chief marketing officer of Tableau, shared the authentically human aspect of what makes their community culture so special:

> In the early days, we went to a lot of effort to make sure that people knew each other as people. So we took a lot of energy and time into making sure that our people that touched the community were personal too. We really tried to imbibe a sense of the personal, that people are human. They like to laugh, they like to join in, they like to be personal.

What authentically binds the humans in your community together?

Determine What Your Community Stands For

Now that you've created values for your community, it's time to canonize a purpose. What does your group stand for? What is their calling?

In the Pulse community, nominally members share a profession—customer success management. But more broadly, they share an ideal. They believe that it is possible to have win-win relationships, where vendors and customers both win. They are passionate about creating success for all of their stakeholders. At the most fundamental level, Pulse members believe in "Human-First Business," the idea that behind our roles as vendors, customers, employees, and the like, we are all just human beings.

This shows up in many ways in Pulse:

- Pulse members have created programs, under the name Pulse Impact, to bring more diversity and equality into the profession.
- They constantly push the envelope on what they can do to drive value for their clients.

■ They passionately advocate inside their companies on behalf of their customers.

Take a moment to reflect on business events you have attended. Did any of them move you on an emotional level? Did they evoke a sense of purpose within you? Did you feel part of a community? Events that do this hold a remarkable ability to leave a lasting impact on attendees. They ignite a collective passion and drive. Recognize the power of purpose. This shared sense of purpose makes a community more than a tactical way to get your job done. Purpose-aligned communities create engagement and impact like no others.

What is the purpose of your community?

Identify and Embrace Your Community's Authentic Quirks

Our virtues aren't the only things that bind us together. We'd argue that quirks and flaws are equally important to the process of making connections. How do the members of your community stand out in a less-flattering way? What makes them lovably weird?

Being in the customer success profession, Pulse attendees tend to be people pleasers. While they are constantly growing and developing their skills, they commiserate over not being understood by their peers at their companies. They joke about their never-ending pattern of taking on too much with their clients. And they have a significant penchant for karaoke.

Erica Kuhl from Salesforce says "quirks" were a core part of their community culture:

> I had one community member that was answering a massive amount of questions. Steve was balancing almost the entire community, in its early days, on his answers alone. When he told me he was going on vacation, I fully panicked. I was like, "Oh no, what is going to go on with my community when he goes on vacation?" And I said, "Well, I'm going to benchmark this moment and see his impact when he's gone."
>
> And it was massive. And when he got back, I was thinking to myself, okay, I got to do a better job of creating more Steves. That's fundamentally on me, but I need to do something incredible for him because of the

impact that he has on our community. So he's from Boston. He loves beer, and in particular, Pliny the Elder, which is a Russian River Brewing cult beer. He loves it, but can't get it in Massachusetts. And this is not exactly legal what I'm about to tell you, but I don't care.

I went and bought Pliny the Elder bombers at Whole Foods. I packaged them up, and I learned how to send marinades through the mail. I dry-iced them, and I shipped them to Boston. So he got them and he is still the top performer in the community today. I've now left Salesforce three years ago, we're almost 20 years on. And he will tell you it's because of these connections and this personalization that we had from the very beginning that he is still part of it. So I love that backstory.

Elissa Fink from Tableau shared some fun stories with us about their quirky community:

We had this one community member that started their own awards. They called them The Vizzies. As an example, and I'm a little shy about it, because it's about me, but they had an award based upon me. I'm known to swear. And they had this award that was the Elissa Fink swearing award. If you would do a visualization with swearing, you got the award.

Another time, one of our super-engaged employees, who I would almost call a community member first and an employee second, made up this dance, and it was The Viz dance. And she put it in the blog and put it on a bunch of other sites, and all of a sudden, everybody was doing it. And when we did the conference a few months later, they had a flash mob in the exhibit hall of, I'd say, I don't know, 200 to 250 people.

Another one, just for fun, was when we launched version six of our software, we did a marketing campaign called the Joy of Six. We encouraged our community to participate. They posted jokes on Twitter like "I told my wife I'd be home late because I was having Six at work."

How does your community stand out?

Build a Brand and Voice for Your Community

Armed with values, purpose, and quirks, it's time to canonize your community with a brand. What are some emotional ways to reinforce the common connection your members share?

A term is a start. As we've discussed, we use the term "Human-First" to capture the spirit of Pulse. But while a pithy purpose or mission statement is great, a picture is worth a thousand words. And if that's true, a parody video might be worth many more. At Gainsight, we've created a shocking number of YouTube clips that use humor to capture the feeling of the Pulse community. These include:

- A Taylor Swift parody of "Blank Space" chronicling the daily life of a customer success manager
- A country music song covering Garth Brooks's "Friends in Low Places" about the hard parts of supporting customers
- A Back Street Boys homage to "I Want It That Way" about clients forcing you to build the product to fit only their needs
- A Disney-themed musical chronicling the phases of a customer relationship
- A Ted Lasso parody all about the unique learnings involved in leading a customer success team
- And, of course, a rap video

It's time to get creative. How can you leverage the power of your right brain to find ways to capture the spirit of your community?

Use Vulnerability to Open People Up

Communities are reinforcing. If some people show up inauthentically, others will follow and put up walls. But if the first to speak and interact truly opens up, the logjam will break and people will get real.

As a community organizer, you have an opportunity to set the tone. Whether it's your first posts online or your first words at a conference, what you say, people will follow. If you start by talking about how great you are, your members will feel like they need to posture as well. But if you open up with authenticity, you'll find that it's infectious.

No one has done more to advocate for leading with vulnerability than best-selling author and TED Talk sensation Brené Brown. Brown makes the claim that while admitting weaknesses and doubts was historically eschewed in the chest-pounding of leadership, the most respected and powerful leaders are the ones who truly open up.

In our Pulse events, we've consistently tried to set this tone. Famously, Nick's closing keynote is year-over-year an attempt to break the armor that keeps us apart. Nick has spoken at successive events about:

- Feelings of not being "enough," no matter how much success we all have
- His childhood loneliness and how it's with him to this day
- His children and how they share this isolation from time to time
- His father's dementia and how it's made him appreciate each moment that much more

And we aren't alone. Vulnerability is an important facet of nearly every community that we've studied. How can you be brave and show up honestly to your community? How can you start a virtuous cycle of vulnerability?

Conclusion

We trust the examples provided gave you some tips to think about when defining your culture. We hope we have also convinced you that breaking the walls between your company culture, brand, and community culture is a critical final step in building a successful community.

This concludes the final law and Part II of this book. The 10 Laws of Community provide you with all the essential strategic building blocks for getting your community strategy right. In Part III, we will continue with practical advice on how to get started with a great community program and how to overcome internal hurdles.

PART

III

How to Get Started

15 | Building Blocks to Successfully Starting a Community

Putting Together a Strong Strategy in Five Steps

In the first two parts of this book, we've covered many of the most essential principles that relate to building an effective community. Now it's worthwhile reflecting on the process of actually putting it all together and creating a community strategy. We've seen countless community strategies over the years, and many of them share similar themes. We will, in fact, share a strategy template that includes many of the most common themes that likely will play a role in getting your community off the ground. Such a template can provide useful inspiration, but before we share that, let's first talk about a very common pitfall.

When we ask customers what they want to achieve with their community, they will often say something like, "We want it to be a community of practice," or "We want our customers to connect with each other and get inspired." Those are fine answers, but sometimes it turns out that what is being aimed for isn't happening. Perhaps the community isn't growing as expected. Or perhaps something else unexpected is happening. It's not uncommon, for example, to hear from a community team that they don't want to have a support-focused community but somehow their community members keep asking support questions. They then might wonder how to make this stop. Very often, the pitfall that these teams have fallen into is that they have taken a mostly inside-out perspective of the community. They have defined a community concept and a direction but haven't taken into account all of the factors and the unique context that surrounds their company, their product, and their customers. Also, they likely haven't defined a clear goal or true purpose for the community that is aligned with their business objectives. Let's unpack this and walk through a step-by-step process that avoids these traps.

Step 1: Determine Your Goals and Priorities and Map Them to Community Use Cases

A community needs to serve a purpose. And that purpose can ultimately touch on a number of different community use cases. In Chapter 4, we discussed how your customer success, marketing, product, and sales organizations can all benefit from your community program. We sometimes use the breakdown seen here to illustrate how that cross-organizational value looks in terms of the five most common use cases and their related metrics and activities.

	Service and P2P Support	Education and Inspiration	Advocacy	Networking and Connection	Product Ideas and Updates
Modules	Community Knowledge Base	Community Knowledge Base Events	Conversations Group Events	Group Events	Ideas Product Updated
Metrics	Self-service ratio, deflection, answers by peer	Content helpfulness, event attendance and survey feedback	Event attendance, Group membership and participation	Event attendance and survey feedback, Group membership and participation	Ideas and votes, ideas and votes delivered
Activities and Focus	Moderation, gamification, KB content, superuser engagement	KB content (articles), webinars, guest contributors	Webinars, events and group facilitation	Event attendance and survey feedback, group membership and participation	Idea follow-ups, publishing product updates
Supporting Platforms	Support portal, video hosting platform	Video hosting platform, webinar platform, LMS	Advocacy and incentives platform, webinar platform	Webinar platform	Roadmap platform

When building a community in the B2B SaaS space, we actually recommend considering all of these use cases, as they are likely all going to be relevant and valuable for your business. However, it's seldom a good idea to try to do everything all at once, right from the start. Instead, we recommend you consider what the primary business problems and opportunities are, and then map them to these use cases to determine the primary focus of the community. For example, you may be in a situation where you most urgently need to scale your support organization and improve the product feedback loop in order to drive more product adoption and satisfaction. This gives you a good starting point for where to focus your efforts in the first few months. It will increase the likelihood that you will see early success and value, particularly if you are focusing on real business outcomes, as we recommended in Law 9.

So far, this is all very much common sense. The pitfall we mentioned above, however, would be to stop here. So let's reflect on the other important factors that must be taken into account.

Step 2: Understand Your Audience and Key Personas

Having determined where you want to focus your initial community efforts, it's a good idea to reflect on the unique nature of your audience. As we discussed in Law 4, your company has likely already defined the key personas that make up your audience, so you can draw on those insights. Here are three simple example questions that we recommend exploring, to start with:

1. What is the size of your audience and what are the key personas?
2. What kind of relationship do they have with your product?
3. What are their biggest needs and challenges related to your product?

Each of these questions is likely to provide insight into the unique situation you're in and what kind of community strategy is going to work for you. For example, the size of your audience will tell you something about how easy it will be to reach critical mass and organic growth in terms of ongoing engagement. If you have only 100 or 200 customers in total, with perhaps just one or two active users of your product per company, your strategy is going to need to include consistent proactive efforts to engage this audience. Similarly, the nature of their relationship with your product will also inform your strategy. If your customers spend an hour or two per week engaging with your product you will be in a very different situation than if your customers work with your product all day, every day.

The third question about what your customers need is probably the most essential one. It seems an obvious consideration, but it's very often missed. To get a community strategy right, we really do need to know and understand our audience and what they need and want the most. Do they have a lot of technical challenges? Are they mostly running into "how-to" questions and looking for best practices? Do they have a lot of product ideas? Are they looking to network and develop their careers? This is where we are able to sanity-check the focus areas we defined in step 1, because what we want to do with the community has to match the needs of our audience. Not reflecting on this sufficiently is how some community teams are surprised that they have ended up with a support-focused community when that wasn't their goal at all. In the end, your customers will show you with their behavior what they want and expect from the community.

In order to gain a deeper understanding of your audience, it is a good idea to pull in data and insights. For example, what are the top 10 questions that get asked of the support team? What are the main churn reasons? What are the top success factors? What are the biggest challenges that the customer success team runs into with their customers? And if you're able to, one of the absolute most powerful things to do is to actually set up some customer interviews, or perhaps send out a survey. This will likely give you deep insights that you can directly apply to your community strategy in terms of where to focus your content creation and engagement, as well as where the most effort is going to be needed to meet the needs of your audience. And it can be the start of your engagement and actually building a community.

Step 3: Reflect on Your Organization and Culture

We now know where we want to focus our efforts and we have validated that we understand our audience and their needs. Now let's consider another factor that often isn't sufficiently taken into account—your unique company culture. We talked about culture extensively in Law 10, and how to bring your culture and values to your community. Here we will discuss how to take your organization and culture into account while building your community strategy and execution plan. Let's reflect by using a few example questions:

1. How risk-averse is your organization?
2. Can you experiment or do you need to prove value quickly?
3. How does your organization look at value?

The community strategy that works for you will be one that is compatible and dialed-in to your organization's unique culture. If your company is highly risk-averse, you will likely need a methodical plan that carefully progresses through measured incremental steps. Or, on the opposite side of this scale, you might find that your best strategy may be to be bold, move fast, and experiment, seeing every failure as a learning to embrace. There is no right or wrong answer here;

it depends on your culture and what will resonate and work in your organization.

In step 1, we reflected on the business problems and opportunities that we want to focus on. It's a good idea to also reflect on how your organization thinks and talks about value. Do you need to produce a robust ROI model that demonstrates clear financial gains or cost savings? Or does your leadership team and wider organization understand the intrinsic value of community engagement, and respond better to storytelling and demonstrations of customer intimacy? These nuances can helpfully inform how you think about your metrics and KPIs, and of course we recommend making use of some of the best practices we outlined in Law 9.

Step 4: Consider Your Ecosystem

Your community does not exist in a vacuum. It's going to be part of a broader ecosystem of tools, channels, and touchpoints. The nature of this overall ecosystem is something that you need to take into account in order to determine the unique purpose and strategy of your community.

Here are three example questions to reflect on:

1. What other resources does your audience have access to and where do they engage with each other today?
2. How will you (be able to) position your community in the ecosystem?
3. What is the unique purpose of your community within this ecosystem?

In step 2, we reflected on the needs of your audience. That's an important question, but we also need to consider what other touchpoints might be fulfilling those needs today, and thereby potentially competing with the goals you have set out for your community. For example, it's possible that your audience has a strong drive to network but that they are relatively comfortably meeting their needs on LinkedIn or in a Slack group. The first step might then be to reflect on whether networking is going to be a primary focus of your community. In order to successfully adopt this use case as part of your community program, you would need to ensure that you are offering something that is lower effort than what already exists or something that adds additional value, otherwise this use case will not gain traction. Your community might, for example, host unique groups and events to facilitate networking that doesn't exist anywhere else. And to take it further, you may need to consider ways to tap into those existing touchpoints and create connections and cross-links to your community.

These questions will help you determine what purposes your community is going to fulfill that aren't being (fully) fulfilled somewhere else. This is important to the long-term success of your community as members will come back when the community has a clear purpose and is meeting a need that isn't getting met somewhere else.

As an example, one of the questions we commonly encounter is about how to drive a support-focused use case alongside a knowledge-based portal. As we discussed in Law 3, we believe in the vision of a community that is integrated into the customer journey. And in Law 8, we discussed the community acting as a central hub and primary landing page as the ideal approach. Nevertheless, we may find that there are touchpoints that serve a similar purpose, such as a knowledge-based portal living alongside the community. In such a case, we should reflect on what the difference really is. For example, we might determine that the community also serves a support function, but that it emphasizes best practice and "how-to" content (see Law 4), which isn't represented in the knowledge-based portal. Once your community's purpose has been clarified in this way, it will inform your strategy and give you direction into how you can best represent your community within the customer journey as well as in your storytelling to your organization.

Step 5: Compile Your Learnings into a Community Strategy and Action Plan

In the steps above we have taken a holistic approach to understanding the key factors around your company, audience, and ecosystem. With these learnings, you are now able to thoughtfully construct your community strategy in a way that is likely to get great results.

One of our favorite ways of summarizing a community strategy, in particular, when creating a plan for a full year or longer, is using the OGSM framework (objective, goals, strategies, measures); for shorter time frames, such as quarters, working with Objectives and Key Results (OKRs) can be more useful. There are many resources online around how to work with OGSM so we won't go deeply into the methodology itself here, but the essence is quite simple—you compile your objective, goals, strategies, and measures in a clean one-page overview.

Here is a very simple template for a community plan that uses the OGSM framework, including examples of common strategic themes. One level lower you would also have a set of specific tactics (with timelines) tied to each of the strategies. Together, these would make up your complete plan and roadmap. Make sure to tie your plan to a set of concrete actions and tactics with timelines and owners.

Objective: *Your community objective for this timeframe in one sentence*	
Goals and Measures	**Strategies**
Your first goal and KPIs, for example, around **support and self-service**	*Your first strategy, for example, around the* **positioning of the community and promotion**
Your second goal and KPIs, for example, around **engagement and advocacy**	*Your second strategy, for example, around* **content planning and creation**
	Your third strategy, for example, around **driving engagement and advocacy**
Your third goal and KPIs, for example, around **product feedback**	*Your fourth strategy, for example, around* **data and insights**
	Your fifth strategy, for example, around **optimizing your platform and integrations**

What to Expect in Your First Year

Launching a new community can be exciting as well as daunting. We commonly hear questions such as "How much traffic should we be getting?" or "Are we getting enough members?" It's natural to wonder how you're doing in comparison to other communities. With our customers, we regularly develop benchmark data that tells some of this story. But those numbers are in themselves always limited, as they don't take into account the unique situation of your community. As Tyler McNally, Gainsight's SVP of CS experience and operations, likes to say when a question comes up around benchmarks, "What's a good NPS? One that is going up over time. And one where you're actively addressing the root causes behind your current score."

So instead of focusing on benchmarks, it can be much more helpful to think about navigating your community through stages of maturity across a number of themes. There are many ways we can think about community maturity, but the simplest and most common one to consider is a breakdown with a series of fundamental phases. Let's look at a simplified version.

Typical B2B SaaS Community Maturity Phases

INTEGRATED
- WHO Company-wide
- WHAT Customer engagement core to business operations
- HOW Cross-functional adoption of all use cases and community mindset
- KPIs Multiple business outcomes

MATURITY
- WHO CS & product & marketing
- WHAT Deep engagement
- HOW Peer-to-peer, advocate program, events, product feedback loop
- KPIs Organic traffic, P2P, business outcomes

ADOPTION
- WHO CS team
- WHAT Effective and healthy community
- HOW Moderation, Q&A, best answers, content
- KPIs Topics with no replies, best answers, helpfulness

LAUNCHING
- WHO Small pioneering team or individual
- WHAT Successful launch and foundation for growth
- HOW Central destination for self-service
- KPIs Unique visitors, new registrations, posts

Using a simplified model like this can be helpful in terms of identifying where you are on your journey, whether that's at the beginning with a small-scale renegade initiative to lay the foundations of a new program, or at a highly mature phase where the program is part of your company's culture and DNA. Or, more likely, like most companies, you are somewhere in the middle.

The Four Quadrants of Community Maturity

The challenge with these kinds of "phase" models is that they don't capture the nuances of where you are in different areas and don't surface actionable insight into what you should focus on next. To address this, we sometimes work with what we call a four-quadrant model of maturity. This model splits maturity into four themes:

1. **Organization.** How advanced is your organization when it comes to the community program? Is it deeply embedded across multiple organizations, and do you have the dedicated resources needed to make it successful?
2. **Processes.** Have you established all the critical processes that are needed to deliver a successful community program?
3. **Adoption of use cases.** As we have mentioned throughout this book, for B2B SaaS communities we recommend adopting a broad set of use cases. How far are you on this journey?
4. **Integrations.** A community can't succeed as a silo. How well integrated and embedded is your community in the customer journey and in your technology stack?

A simple way to work with this model is to ask yourself the following seven questions for each quadrant. This will give you an initial score, but more importantly, it will give you clues as to which areas to focus on next.

1 ORGANIZATION

1. Do you have a community manager in place to lead your efforts?
2. Do you have moderation in place to monitor community content on a daily basis?
3. Do you have an executive champion?
4. Is the community program embedded within customer success?
5. Is the community program embedded within marketing?
6. Is the community program embedded within support?
7. Is the community program embedded within product?

2 ADOPTION OF USE CASES

1. Are you utilizing the community for Q&A and support-focused content?
2. Are you utilizing the community for the sharing of educational and inspirational content?
3. Are you using groups and events to facilitate networking and connection between members?
4. Are you capturing product feedback and closing the loop by communicating releases in the community?
5. Are you actively driving advocacy through the community?
6. Are you reaching all your key personas with your current use cases?
7. Are you reaching all of your customers?

3 PROCESSES

1. Do you have a clear and consistent moderation process?
2. Do you have a roadmap of initiatives and metrics?
3. Do you regularly share a report with community data, insights, and success stories within your business?
4. Do you have a community content calendar?
5. Do you have a process to identify and engage with top community members?
6. Do you have an internal process to manage the product feedback loop?
7. Do you have a regular meeting cadence with senior leadership to discuss the community program?

4 INTEGRATIONS

1. Is your community a central landing page where your customers can find all useful resources?
2. Are you leveraging federated search?
3. Do you have Single Sign-On (SSO) enabled?
4. Are you embedding community content in your product or website?
5. Have you integrated community with your CRM system?
6. Have you integrated community with your ticketing system?
7. Are you developing automations via Zapier and/or API?

Possible answers for all questions: **YES** (1 point) | **SOMEWHAT** (0.5 POINTS) | **NO** (0 points)

You're Excited to Get Started but Someone Else Isn't?

Hopefully by now you're excited about the value that a customer community can bring to your company and you have a lot of ideas about how to put together your strategy and action plan. We know from experience, however, that sometimes you will get pushback from others in your organization. Luckily, what we've found over the years is that pushback tends to come in the form of a few extremely common objections that are rooted in a lack of experience with community engagement and some understandable initial concerns stemming from that. In the next chapter, we'll walk you through the most common objections and share effective ways of countering them, thereby getting the buy-in that you need.

16

Common Objections and How to Overcome Them

Answers to Nine Common Objections

As with every big change and new initiative, starting a community will bring both excitement and anxiety. While you may have read this book, have your strategy (almost) ready, and have full trust in its success, others may have doubts and questions.

For community practitioners who are exploring the idea of starting a community, our first recommendation is to get your business leaders on the same page in terms of strategic talking points. Give a copy of this book to your leadership team, your heads of support, customer success, marketing, and product. Follow up with them to make sure the central concepts are understood. This will help you to gain that broad alignment that you want and will help to avoid misalignment down the road.

Even with the best preparation and communication, however, you may get some doubts or objections regarding your initiative. Most objections are related to value, resources, time, organizational buy-in, and risks. If someone has an objection, you can, of course, ask them to read this book, but you'll also want to be able to handle the objection directly. In this chapter, we will walk through some very common objections and how we typically respond to them. Note that almost all of these objections are related to a misunderstanding of how communities work and the value they deliver, so what we're doing here is sharing information and context that everyone doesn't have but can benefit from.

Objection 1: Building a Community Program Is Too Expensive

Building a community takes dedication and resources. But, as we covered in this book and especially in Law 9, the community is there to drive real business outcomes and should be delivering a significant return on investment. So start by defining your desired outcomes and then estimate the budget you would need to achieve them. You can then make a well-reasoned decision. If you're not yet at a place where you can invest in a major community program and owned platform, then consider the smaller ways that you can get started with community building that we discussed in Law 1.

Objection 2: We Don't Have the Resources to Build a Community

A common misconception for first-time community builders (and buyers) is that it takes a lot of resources to build a community. While it is a common best practice for mature programs to have dedicated full-time employees driving the community program (usually a community manager and potentially moderators and some other specialized roles), we also see companies effectively get started with responsibilities dispersed across a few individuals. In practice, it might mean that a handful of people invest a few hours per week into the program to get started. As the program gains traction, grows, and delivers value over time, it can then organically evolve toward having dedicated full-time resources.

Objection 3: I Don't Have Time to Build and Manage a Community

Best-in-class companies hire a full-time community employee to manage and moderate the community on a day-to-day basis: the community manager. When your company doesn't have a community manager (because of budget, because you're still hiring, or because you first want to see if the community project adds value), it will be an additional role for someone to fulfill and it may seem overwhelming and time-consuming.

We're not going to lie: building and managing a community does take time. But the time you invest in the community is time well spent and you'll reap returns in the long run. Let's take a look at an example. How much time are you spending on a daily basis answering repetitive questions? Consider using the same time to write a community article that provides an in-depth answer to the question. Next time you can simply point users to the community article instead of answering the question in a one-to-one way, thus saving you several hours. What's more, a community article allows the rest of the community to provide feedback, making it even more comprehensive and better over time.

Objection 4: Sounds Great, but We Have Other Priorities

Within every company there are more plans and ideas than resources. Prioritizing is one of the key factors to building a successful business. Therefore, organizational frameworks like yearly planning sessions, OKRs, and OGSMs are mission-critical. So if someone states there are other priorities, basically they are saying that other projects have a better value versus effort tradeoff. If you get this objection, try to find common ground on the value and effort of the community program. Then discuss where this project should be on the priority list. And in case there are indeed other priorities, try to make your initiative smaller. After all, as we mentioned in Law 1, you can start anytime, even with small initiatives.

Objection 5: The Rest of the Organization Is Not Convinced

Communities can touch multiple layers and teams of the organization: customer success, customer support, marketing, and product. Not everybody in the organization might see the value of a community, often because other stakeholders assume the cost is higher than the benefit.

Make time to meet with other departments, ask them what they are concerned about, and show them what value a community can bring to their department. Some common examples we see are:

- Support teams benefit from a community because it reduces the volume of support tickets. It helps them focus on value-add interactions as the community handles the most common and simple questions.
- Customer success teams benefit from a community because it helps them scale their digital CS efforts by creating a place where customers can connect with and learn from each other, as opposed to only learning from their CSM.
- Marketing teams often struggle to find speakers and create great case studies. These customers naturally present themselves in the community as the top members and advocates.
- Product teams gain huge efficiencies by aggregating product feedback via the community. They can also directly influence adoption by communicating about new product capabilities.

Objection 6: We Don't Need a Community, Because We Already Have a Knowledge Base/Ticketing System/LMS/Documentation/Product Feedback Tools

It's great if you already have various touchpoints and resources available for your customers, but the community program will offer unique and complementary benefits to everything that exists today. The community is able to act as a central destination that weaves together and surfaces content from all of your helpful resources, thereby healing the fragmented experience that so many B2B SaaS companies suffer from. Additionally, the community will offer a path toward scaling customer engagement and digital customer success by creating a unique place for one-to-many communication, peer-to-peer Q&A, customer education, and so much more.

Objection 7: We're Too Small to Start a Community

It is easier to build an engaging community with a larger customer base, and there is actually a degree of scale needed in order to gain value from an owned community platform. As a very rough guideline, we typically say that your B2B SaaS business will need to have at least 50-100 customers before an owned community platform will truly make sense. However, as we have discussed in this book, you are never too small to start with community-building. Your earliest efforts may simply need to be scaled down to the tactics we described in Law 1, with a greater focus on small meetups and direct engagement with customers. And we recommend doing that from the very beginning, no matter how many or how few customers you have.

If you have a small customer base, we recommend drafting a long-term plan for your business that outlines how your community-building will evolve as you scale. That might mean planning to invest in an owned community platform and program a few years down the road.

Objection 8: I'm Afraid of Negative Feedback

We hear this one very often. Many companies are afraid that their community after launch will be overflooded by negativity. But in all of our years of community building, the fear of a tsunami of negativity has never become a reality for any of our customers. Yes, there will be some negative feedback—it simply means that a customer is unhappy with some part of their experience. Whether or not you have a community, they will be voicing that unhappiness to friends, colleagues, and potentially even on social media channels. Receiving negative feedback on your community is therefore a golden opportunity to be embraced, because it offers you a chance to join the conversation and make things right.

You will always have the "terms and conditions" of your community to fall back on if behavior crosses a line. As long as your members adhere to those principles of good conduct, you can embrace criticism, respond to it, and share it broadly within your company. Communities can be incredible change agents, often within months of launch. Responding to criticism in an authentic way and demonstrating that you are listening will transform the sentiment of unhappy customers. We have, in fact, more than once seen a community's most negative detractor transform into a raving advocate over time.

Objection 9: I'm Afraid That the Competitors Will See (and Steal) Our Content

When you create an online community, you and your customers will be sharing valuable content. As we covered in Laws 3 and 4, this content can be around thought leadership, your product, your vision, best practices, and customer stories. To a certain extent, this indeed does mean that you are opening up to the world and sharing content that will also be available to your competitors. That's the case for any content you share. Your competitors can also see your webinars, your presentations at major events, and your marketing blogs. We have found that the most effective mindset here is to be generous with your best ideas and most valuable content. That's what we have practiced ourselves ever since Gainsight was founded, through our Pulse events, our marketing blogs, social media posts, and the books we publish—like this one! We strongly believe that this open and generous mindset has helped establish Gainsight as the leading authority and thought leader in the customer success space.

That said, there may well be some information that you want to keep private. In your community, you can always restrict access to particular sections. You might, for instance, want your customers to be able to access only the product feedback section. You can even decide to share access only to specific areas after your customers sign an NDA (for beta programs, for example). It's also possible to restrict access to your community entirely so that only your customers can access it after logging in. We usually don't recommend that approach, however, because more open community spaces tend to be more engaging and successful.

Other Objections or Tricky Questions?

It's possible that you will come across objections that we haven't fully covered here, or questions that you don't have the answers to. If that happens we'd like to encourage you to visit our community and ask for help there.

Epilogue

As we come to the end of this book, we find ourselves reflecting on the journey that led us to write about the power of communities. What started as a business project as part of our regular workweek soon transformed into a deeply personal endeavor, enriched by the stories and experiences of individuals who have shaped and been shaped by these vibrant ecosystems.

In our quest to understand the essence of thriving business communities, we had the privilege of connecting with remarkable individuals who shared their journeys and insights. Through their stories, we discovered that beyond the exchange of value, communities are fueled by human-first connections, empathy, and a shared desire for growth and collaboration.

As we delved deeper into the lives of many business executives, we were struck by the profound impact that these communities had on their personal growth. Behind every success story, there were countless individuals who lent a helping hand, provided guidance, and offered unwavering support. It became evident that in the world of business, true success is not solely measured by profit margins, but by the strength of the community relationships we foster along the way.

We've also experienced this ourselves in building Gainsight, where we've seen hundreds of leaders moving up the career ladder due to connections they made throughout our community. In fact, we even had business leaders saying they did not want to send their employees to our Pulse events because they would meet others in the community and might be inclined to change jobs! That is a true testament to how community can power real life-changing events.

As we conclude this journey, we are also reminded of the profound impact communities have had on our own personal lives. The camaraderie, the shared knowledge, and the boundless inspiration we have encountered along the way have left an indelible mark on our own paths as CEOs and business leaders.

May the insights gleaned from this book serve as a guiding light, illuminating your own path to building successful communities, whether that is in your private life or business environment, supporting your family and friends or supporting your customers in their success and fulfillment. Let us remember that our greatest achievements are not measured solely by financial gains but by the impact we have on the lives of others and the legacy we leave behind.

Thank you for joining us on this transformative journey, and may the power of communities continue to flourish, shaping a better human-first future for all.

—Nick Mehta and Robin van Lieshout

References

Chapter 1

Aristotle. *Politics.* Translated by C. D. C. Reeve. Book 1, 1253a. Indianapolis, IN: Hackett Publishing Company, 2017.

Buettner, Dan. "How to Live to Be 100+." Lecture presented at the TEDxTC, September 2, 2009. https://www.youtube.com/watch?v=I-jk9ni4XWk.

Cigna. "Cigna 2018 U.S. Loneliness Index." Cigna Corporation and Ipsos, May 1, 2018. https://www.cigna.com/assets/docs/newsroom/loneliness-survey-2018-updated-fact-sheet.pdf.

Holt-Lunstad, J., D. Stephenson, M. Harris, and T. B. Baker. "Loneliness and Social Isolation as Risk Factors for Mortality: A Meta-Analytic Review." *Perspectives on Psychological Science: A Journal of the Association for Psychological Science.* National Library of Medicine, March 11, 2015. https://pubmed.ncbi.nlm.nih.gov/25910392/.

Murthy, Vivek Hallegere. *Together: The Healing Power of Human Connection in a Sometimes Lonely World.* New York: Harper Wave, an imprint of HarperCollins, 2020.

Oldenburg, Ray. *The Great Good Place: Cafés, Coffee Shops, Community Centers, Beauty Parlors, General Stores, Bars, Hangouts, and How They Get You through the Day.* New York: Paragon House, 1989.

Tomova, Livia, Kimberly L. Wang, Todd Thompson, Gillian A. Matthews, Atsushi Takahashi, Kay M. Tye, and Rebecca Saxe. "Acute Social Isolation Evokes Midbrain Craving Responses Similar to Hunger." *Nature News*. Nature Publishing Group, November 23, 2020. https://www.nature.com/articles/s41593-020-00742-z.

The Godfather. VHS. United States: Paramount Pictures, 1972.

The Office. Season 3, episode 16, "Phyllis' Wedding." February 8, 2007.

Chapter 2

Andreessen, Marc. "Why Software Is Eating the World." *Wall Street Journal.* August 11, 2011. https://www.wsj.com/articles/SB10001424053111903480904576512250915629460.

Bailey, Mckenna. "Why Is NRR Your Most Important Growth Metric?" Gainsight, November 15, 2021. https://www.gainsight.com/blog/nrr-north-star-growth-metric/.

Detroit Historical Society. "Model T." *Encyclopedia of Detroit.* Detroit Historical Society. Accessed April 20, 2023. https://detroithistorical.org/learn/encyclopedia-of-detroit/model-t.

Ethereum. "What Is Web3 and Why Is It Important?" April 19, 2023. https://ethereum.org/en/web3/.

Ford Motor Company. "The Model T." Accessed April 20, 2023 https://corporate.ford.com/articles/history/the-model-t.html.

Hayes, Adam. "The Risks and Rewards of Investing in Startups." Investopedia, July 28, 2022. https://www.investopedia.com/articles/personal-finance/041315/risk-and-rewards-investing-startups.asp.

Konrad, Alex. "The Cloud 100." Bessemer Venture Partners and Salesforce Ventures, August 9, 2022. https://www.forbes.com/lists/cloud100/?sh=730d11987d9c.

Marino, Maria, Michael Maziarka, and Chad Storlie. "Market Guide for B2B Customer Community Platforms." Gartner, October 10, 2022. https://www.gartner.com/en/documents/4004093.

Moore, Geoffrey A. *Crossing the Chasm: Marketing and Selling High-Tech Products to Mainstream Customers*. New York: HarperBusiness Essentials, 2014.

Pattabhiram, Chandar. "The 'C' Shift to Becoming a MegaBrand." LinkedIn, December 19, 2019. https://www.linkedin.com/pulse/c-shift-becoming-megabrand-chandar-pattabhiram.

Shah, Dharmesh. "INBOUND 2022." HubSpot Marketing, 2022. https://www.youtube.com/watch?v=0PvZTD6oEBc&t=4s.

Vaidyanathan, Ashvin, and Ruben Rabago. Essay, in *The Customer Success Professional's Handbook: How to Thrive in One of the World's Fastest Growing Careers—While Driving Growth for Your Company*. Hoboken, NJ: John Wiley & Sons, 2020, pp. 138–138.

Walker, Kate, and Talia Goldberg. "Five Laws for Community-Led Growth." Bessemer Venture Partners, August 16, 2022. https://www.bvp.com/atlas/five-laws-for-community-led-growth.

Chapter 3

Marino, Maria, Michael Maziarka, and Chad Storlie. "Market Guide for B2B Customer Community Platforms." Gartner, October 10, 2022. https://www.gartner.com/en/documents/4004093.

Chapter 4

Bickart, Barbara, and Robert M. Schindler. "Internet Forums as Influential Sources of Consumer Information." *Journal of Interactive Marketing* 15, no. 3 (June 28, 2001): 31–40. doi:10.1002/dir.1014.abs.

Chen, Chun-Der, and Edward C. Ku. "Diversified Online Review Websites as Accelerators for Online Impulsive Buying: The Moderating Effect of Price Dispersion." *Journal of Internet Commerce* 20, no. 1 (January 2, 2021): 113–35. doi:10.1080/15332861.2020.1868227.

Constantinides, Efthymios, and Nina Isabel Holleschovsky. "Impact of Online Product Reviews on Purchasing Decisions." *Proceedings of the 12th International Conference on Web Information Systems and Technologies* 2 (April 23, 2016): 271–78. doi:10.5220/0005861002710278.

Marmon, Johanna. "Why We Care about Search Marketing." *Mar-Tech*, March 28, 2023. https://martech.org/why-we-care-about-search-marketing/.

Chapter 7

Imhoff, Claudia, Jonathan G. Geiger, and Lisa Loftis. "Building the Customer-Centric Enterprise, Part 1." *DM Review* 10 (2000): 24–29.

Chapter 10

Magwaza, Pam. "The Community-Led Show #7: Alteryx's Dean Stoecker Means Business with Community." *Commsor*, June 6, 2022. https://www.commsor.com/post/the-community-led-show-7-alteryxs-dean-stoecker-means-business-with-community.

Millington, Richard. *Buzzing Communities: How to Build Bigger, Better, and More Active Online Communities*. FeverBee, 2012.

Chapter 12

Salesforce. *State of the Connected Customer* 2022. https://www.salesforce.com/resources/research-reports/state-of-the-connected-customer/.

Torres, Teresa. *Continuous Discovery Habits: Discover Products That Create Customer Value and Business Value*. Bend, OR: Product Talk LLC, 2021.

Williams, Evan. "Own the Moment of Customer Onboarding: Launch the Love." *Gainsight*, June 29, 2022. https://www.gainsight.com/blog/owning-customer-onboarding-gainsight-essentials/.

Chapter 13

Gothelf, Jeff, and Josh Seiden. "You Need to Manage Digital Projects for Outcomes, Not Outputs." *Harvard Business Review*, February 6, 2017. https://hbr.org/2017/02/you-need-to-manage-digital-projects-for-outcomes-not-outputs.

Quick, Daniel. "Pulse 2022." *In 5 Steps to Measuring the Impact of Customer Education*. San Francisco: Gainsight, August 17, 2022.

Chapter 14

Community Roundtable. "The State of Community Management 2022." https://communityroundtable.com/what-we-do/research/the-state-of-community-management/state-of-community-management-2022/.

"Culture." *Oxford Learner's Dictionary*. Oxford University Press, n.d. https://www.oxfordlearnersdictionaries.com/us/definition/american_english/culture_1.

Jaques, Elliot. *The Changing Culture of a Factory*. London: Tavistock Publications, 1957.

McCord, Patty. *Powerful: Building a Culture of Freedom and Responsibility*. San Francisco: Missionday, 2020.

Hastings, Reed, and Erin Meyer. *No Rules Rules: Netflix and the Culture of Reinvention*. New York: Penguin Press, 2020.

Index